Praise for *Winning Without Compromising...Yourself*

"Finally – a book that helps you achieve political success while keeping your life in balance. If all public officials adhered to the principles put forth in this work our country's political system would be in much better shape. An easy and fun read that holds your attention while teaching important lessons. A must read for anyone considering a run for public office."
— Dr. Kendra Stewart, *Eastern Kentucky University, Department of Government*

"Leadership is responsible service to the people. This service is based on core principles and values. It is the leader's responsibility to know, understand, protect and promote these principles and values in the interest of the nation and its people. Leaders must be visionary and act with courage, to be out front and to lead. This book will guide you to those perspectives and values."
— Oren Lyons, Faithkeeper, *Turtle Clan, Onondaga Nation Council of Chiefs*

"Having worked with hundreds of elected officials and candidates, I can say this book should be read by all visionary leaders seeking or in office. It provides great insights and tools for how to be an extraordinary leader."
—Kelly Young, President, *21st Century Democrats*

"Winning Without Compromising...Yourself gives remarkable insights and practical steps for helping a leader become a transformational leader — someone with courage who can inspire and bring people together to reach common goals. If you want ideas on how to do your leadership job better, you'll be interested in the ideas and practical tips these guides offer."
— Andy Brack, *President, Center for a Better South*

"The political arena receives enormous media attention, much of it negative. Very little help comes from dedicated professionals seeking to assist elected officials to function better. This book is a treasured gift. It assembles extremely insightful information from skilled practitioners of coaching. All who aspire to maximize their contribution in the public arena will find significant value in this book."
— Jack Zenger, CEO of Zenger/Folkman and co-author of the best-selling book *The Extraordinary Leader: Turning good managers into great leaders*

"This book is important and timely. Activists, candidates and public officials alike will benefit from its powerful insights, its clear tone, and its moral imperative that together, we will restore the promise of our country."
— Eric Garcetti, President, *The Los Angeles City Council*

"Politicians today are under monumental pressure to solve problems that most citizens have not even heard of just a few short years ago. Winning Without Compromising.....Yourself *will help any political leader face these complex and challenging issues by bringing the best of themselves to public service. Their coaching found in these pages is bold and fresh and gives us hope that a new political story is in the making."*
— Donna Zajonc, Author, *Politics of Hope: Reviving the Dream of Democracy* and Co-Founder, *Bainbridge Leadership Center*

"John F. Kennedy's Pulitzer Prize-winning book Profiles in Courage *was a very short volume. Truth is, there aren't many fiercely courageous candidates who can fulfill the mandates of their conscience and actually get elected. Perhaps this will now change with the publication of* Winning Without Compromising…Yourself. *There are indeed ways to thread the needles of conviction and victory simultaneously, and this book shows how."*
— Dr. Larry J. Sabato, *University of VA Center for Politics*

"This book is a terrific manual for political leaders who are willing to be 'learners'. It is easy, but so unwise, for leaders to surround themselves with fawning 'yes-men'. Hiring a coach to supply the other side of the coin can turn their lives around, both professionally and personally, if they choose to take that first step."
— Deborah Grey, *Member of Parliament (Ret'd)*

"What have we here? An inspiring book about politics from a place of heartfelt integrity? I'm surely voting for that!"
— Dr. Ron Hulnick, President, *University of Santa Monica*

Winning Without Compromising...Yourself

*Unlocking personal and professional mastery
in the political arena*

www.nocompromising.com

Salon Press

Winning Without Compromising...Yourself
Copyright © 2008 by Salon Press
All rights reserved.

Published by:
Salon Press
PO Box 671
Morgan Hill, CA 95038

in conjunction with

UNITED WRITERS PRESS, INC.
P.O. BOX 326
TUCKER, GEORGIA 30085

ISBN-13: 978-1-934216-34-7
ISBN-10: 1-934216-34-8

Cover Design by Ana Carini
Editing by Kay duPont
Project Management by Kelly Johnson
Interior book design by United Writers Press, Inc.

Publisher's Note:

Table of Contents

Acknowledgments

We have many people to thank for the creation of this book, which was made possible by a virtual, distributed and deeply-committed team.

Kelly Johnson, our virtual assistant, was both patient and effective in herding the cats that spanned a continent and four time zones. Our editor, Kay duPont let us keep our own voices, while making sure our words made sense. The team at Salon Press played a vital role in making our achievement possible.

This work was inspired by many, to whom we are very grateful. Special thanks go to the following people who directly touched this book and supported its realization and accuracy: Delorese Ambrose, Dr. John Bennett, David Bernstein, National Security Advisor to the Prime Minister and Associate Secretary to the Cabinet Margaret Bloodworth, Assistant Chief Deputy Office of Los Angeles County Supervisor Yvonne Burke Chuck Bookhammer, Elliott Brack, Beth Broderick, Wayne Caskey, Michael Corbett, Matthew Driscoll, Robyn Emerson, James Flaherty, Los Angeles City Council President Eric Garcetti, Retired Member of Parliament Deborah Grey, Former Gwinnett County Commission Chairman Wayne Hill, Professor Margaret Holt, Susan Klein, Diana Beresford, Chris Kroeger, Former US Rep. Steve Kuykendall, Francois Leduc, Minnesota Representative John Lesch, Chief Oren Lyons, Sheila Macleod, Melissa O'Mara, Eric Randall, Professor Edward Rogoff, David Schmaltz, Canadian Senator Hugh Segal, Field Deputy Office of Council President Eric Garcetti, Kabira Stokes, Peter Teichroeb, Jack Zenger. And to our families for their loving support, and respect for this great passion of ours.

Thank you.

Introduction

We wrote this book because we want you to win! To deliver on your courageous vision and to improve people's lives for generations to come. To create the space to reflect and thrive within the whirlwind of political life. To be at your best with your family and friends—even when the legislature is in session. To find your most effective balance of leadership styles—say, between nice and pushy. To master personal sustainability so that you're fully expressed and enthusiastically playing in the political arena for a long time to come.

The ideas in this book will contribute vitally to your lasting personal competitive advantage. Exercises to apply the insights are provided throughout the book and some chapters even take workbook form. For those who really work the concepts in this book, the benefits are tremendous. You will:

- become more powerful in yourself,
- feel renewed passion for your job,
- expand healthy confidence,
- trust your decisions more,
- become more self-aware and break habits that aren't serving you, and
- have breakthroughs in areas where you may currently find yourself stuck.

So, how do you find the time to read it? We designed this book to fit the pressures on your time. Each chapter takes a few minutes to read and can stand alone. We recommend keeping the book on your nightstand to start your day with some fresh insights and inspiration. You'll get more out of the book if you do the exercises, and you will still get plenty just reading it alone. Our hope is that you will do what you can and stretch as much as possible. It may take an evening or a month to read; just don't relinquish it to a dusty spot on the bookshelf where it can get lost to the hustle and bustle. Delivering on the promise within you is too important.

Executive Coaching—A Primer

Coaching has long been a tool for the elite. The coaching we're most familiar with is the kind used with sports teams. In fact, John Wooden, the 10-time March Madness NCAA basketball coach, was one of the first to take the techniques that he used on the court and apply them to his work with CEOs. In the last 10 years, executive coaching has become essential to corporate life and is now an established requirement for many executives.

In a recent study, 71% of senior executives and 43% of CEO's in North America are currently working with coaches. Coaching speeds up professional development, is steeped in personal sustainability and shines a light in the dark places where fears and doubts quietly run the show.

As *Fast Company* wrote, "If coaches have one thing in common, it's that they're ruthlessly results oriented. Coaching isn't therapy. It's product development, with you as the product."

Coaching is how you win the inner game of politics—the game within the mind of the player. The outer game is tended by consultants and strategists who serve up technique and push valuable expert advice.

Here's a way to consider the differences.

Outer Game Consultants & Strategists	Inner Game – The Coach
Focuses on external agendas: polls, funders', the party's, their own	Focuses on the political leaders' agenda
Focuses on *likeability*: i.e. tie color, message delivery, a hug versus a handshake	Focuses on *charisma*: authenticity, presence, values, purpose and passion
Invested in the results	Invested in the person
External damage control: spin, counter attacks	Internal damage control: learning, courage, realignment with integrity, purpose and vision
Bases decision-making on external "expert" opinions	Decision-making grounded in personal values and vision, including information from external "expert" opinions — You're the real expert. —
Playing to win by not losing	Playing to win by reaching for the bold vision
Work only focus	Whole-systems approach that cultivates personal sustainability
Focus on doing	Balance of learning and action
Setting goals based on what's possible within existing circumstances — Solutions —	Crafting vision that transforms existing circumstances - Possibilities
Work with clients is a resume booster	Work with clients (including clients' identities) is completely confidential

Reprinted with permission from Glass Houses Coaching & Consulting

The critical aspect that makes coaching possible is an agenda-free and completely confidential environment. Unlike political consultants and pollsters who boast about their clients, coaches do not reveal whom they work for unless arranged otherwise. Absolute confidentiality protects the integrity of the working relationship between client and coach and makes candid conversation possible.

Certified coaches are bound by a set of professional ethics that includes confidentiality and requires them to refrain from any compensation that would be considered a conflict of interest. The focus on the client's agenda is what makes coaching a unique service. What this means in the political arena is that the coach may be the only person who does not want something from the political leader, and never will. Coaches do not bring yet another voice to the process; instead, coaching offers a place to sort through the myriad of conflicting advice with curious inquiry and reflection so your voice rings true. You do this by tapping into deep reserves of integrity, courage, and values in a relationship providing non-critical feedback and genuine support.

Leaders who are unaware of coaching often turn to their staff or family members for this kind of support, which can create conflict. Coaching is a safe place to confide uncertainty, doubt and weakness that could frighten your staff. It's also a secure way to explore ideas that could be threatening to your family. Also, if you are relying on a couple of people for support, they could become overwhelmed and want to start fixing the circumstances you struggle with—or even fixing you.

One benefit coaches with professional training provide is that they are steeped in *supporting* clients as opposed to *helping* them. As an example, *support* is pointing out that you have a hole in your roof and possibly providing ideas and momentum for doing something about it. *Helping*, in contrast, is when someone sees a hole in your roof, grabs a ladder, climbs up with their hammer and boards, and closes the hole. *Helping* may get the hole fixed once, but it's another person's vision of repair, and creates a dependent relationship. The *support* of coaching works consistently with very powerful leaders because of its fundamental basis in learning and development of already capable people.

Some people wonder why able and powerful leaders would find a coach useful. The answer is, that the further leaders advance in their career, the less honest, quality feedback they receive. The coach can act as a three-way mirror, allowing leaders to see themselves and their behavior from fresh perspectives. That helps them see what they look like from outside themselves and glimpse their blind spots. You have to be able to see your current limitations in order to transcend them. A coach will also point out strengths, so they can be fully appreciated and developed. Leaders who step up to coaching are challenged, pushed, celebrated, and held accountable to their promises to themselves. No wonder it works.

On a final note, coaching is not partisan. Coaches coach clients every day who do not share their politics, or share their values. A coach is concerned with *your* values, and how alive and engaged you become when you honor them. This does not mean that coaches cannot be active citizens. It does mean that party politics stop at the water's edge of coaching and the inner game of political leadership.

The Contributors

The essays in this book were contributed by North America's leading coaches in the political arena. Their bios are included after their first essay and collected at the end of the book. The insights they offer come from years of experience coaching elected, appointed and emerging political leaders. And their expertise includes communication, management and delegation, personal leadership, collaboration, and living in the public eye. The authors know the political arena not only through their clients' eyes, but also from their experience as activists, appointees, elected officials, staffers and legislative advisors.

Coaching is a self-regulated profession and the coaches who contributed to this book are committed to the highest standards of ability and conduct. We exhibit this through our extensive coach training, professional certifications and credentials as well as our membership in the International Coach Federation and adherence to its code of ethics (*www.coachfederation.org*).

The authors conduct their coaching in a number of different ways. The majority of coaching happens over the phone, and often conversations can be face-to-face. The most intensive form of coaching is "shadowing" when the coach observes the leader throughout their day to coach for awareness and behavioral change in laser increments, such as between meetings. Coaching can also take the written form of email, and the authors chose this book to offer coaching to you.

We want to see you deliver on your full potential and complete expression of your strengths. We have written this book as a patriotic act to call forth the best political leadership possible—where you can win without compromising...yourself.

Authentic Leadership in the Political Arena: How Do We Recognize It?

Betsy Corley Pickren

Politics is a neutral word. WE determine the meaning. In Webster's dictionary, the first definition of politics is "the science or art of government." The fifth definition is "the use of strategy or intrigue in obtaining power or status." Actually, *politics* is derived from the much juicier Greek word *politeia*, meaning "a civic society carried to its utmost."

To make the last meaning come alive, we depend on our leaders. I have chosen my own criteria for defining the word *politician*. My definition comes from personal experience with an *authentic* political leader.

Authentic political leaders are courageous—they will stand before great powers on behalf of something they believe in.

My work with a program in my church called Advancing Authentic Leadership (AAL) underscored my belief that the search for authenticity as a leader of self and others is a lifelong internal, *spiritual* journey. The leader's journey—any leader—starts within and works its way outward.

Our yearning for true leadership is not a new thing. We even find evidence of it in the Old Testament, when God lamented, *"So I sought for a man among them who would make a wall, and stand in the gap before Me on behalf of the land that I should not destroy it; but I found no one."* (Ezekiel 22:30) We crave leaders who will stand up for their beliefs.

1

Authentic political leaders exert their influence to move a group toward goals that fulfill *real* needs.

John Haggai, founder of the Haggai Institute, wrote in his book, *LEAD ON!*: "Leadership is the discipline of deliberately exerting special influence within a group to move it toward goals of beneficial permanence that fulfill the group's real needs." In my experience, this definition fits perfectly in the political arena.

I have always been fascinated with people in public office. When I was in the 5th grade, I was so adamant about my choice for US President that my friends teased me unmercifully. Even my parents were surprised at my fervor. Being a Southerner at that time meant that almost everyone around me belonged to the Democratic Party. (My, how things have changed!) Adlai Stevenson was challenging President Dwight David Eisenhower for the Presidency. Even though my friends called me *Betsy*, they knew that my real name is *Mamie* Elizabeth. So they gleefully called me *Mamie Eisenhower* at every opportunity. I gave them the emotional reaction they wanted: I lashed out or cried, depending on the day. The difference was that my classmates didn't care who won the election. I did.

Because of that caring, I became curious about politicians and other leaders whose deeply-held beliefs led to "standing in the gap" on behalf of something important. I studied journeys that caused a public figure to move a group toward goals that fulfilled the group's real needs—not the presenting needs. My first example was Minor Morton Corley, a public servant. He was my role model, and he still inspires me. He was my father.

Daddy sat on the Gwinnett County, GA, Board of Commissioners for six years. I campaigned door-to-door in three elections. (Having no brothers or sisters, I enlisted my classmates to campaign with me. You can imagine my passion. Most of the time, people saw me as a kid who idolized her father, and they were very receptive to my message.)

As an elected official, my dad faced a political quandary because of a decision made in the mid-1950s by the former County Commission. They wisely prepared for the future by setting up a water system. In the 1956 election, however, a completely new Commission was swept into office: Uhland Freeman, Dr. W. A. Elinburg Jr. and Gordon Frachiseur. Soon after, Mr. Frachiseur died, and my father, Minor Morton Corley, was elected to fill that seat for the first time.

The problem the new commissioners faced was that there were not enough water customers to satisfy the financial debt on the water system set up by the previous Commission. Foreclosure on the water system by the bondholders seemed imminent. The commissioners saw the need for a water system to fuel the impending growth of the county, but they were between a rock and a hard place. As political leaders who had the power to exert special influence, what must they do?

After being reelected in 1960, the three-man board pondered their options. They could do nothing and let the water system go into bankruptcy. Or they could call on an obscure law that allowed the Board of Commissioners to issue licenses to sell beer. Unfortunately, no one had ever been granted such a license. And, as the news traveled around that the commissioners were contemplating using taxes from the sale of beer to fund the water system, it became clear why there were no beer stores in Gwinnett County.

Gwinnett County is in the heart of the Bible Belt. People argued that the evil of drink was worse than the possibility of losing our water system. I listened to local preachers on the radio attacking my father as a person. People who had been lifetime friends questioned my dad's values. They accused him of being an alcoholic, a non-Christian and more. The fact that at least two adjoining Atlanta metropolitan counties sold alcoholic beverages and a large number of Gwinnett residents trekked across the lines to buy it – leaving their taxes behind – did not seem to occur to the critics. So the dilemma for my dad became one of moving the county toward "goals of beneficial permanence" or giving people who mattered to him personally what they said they wanted. And there was another option: since there were three people on the Board, he could have played it safe. He could choose to be the dissenter and let the other two take the rap for an unpopular decision. But he didn't.

3

Authentic political leaders choose trusted coaches or advisors wisely.

They are confident enough in their own strength to engage in deep conversation with carefully chosen partners who will help them sort through data and values. I vividly remember Daddy's agonizing about the beer-tax decision. Since he was a leader in the Methodist Church, he decided to go to our minister for advice. There were no life coaches or executive coaches at that time. Luckily, the minister seemed to know the tenants of great coaching intuitively.

Reverend J. B. McNeil was at least 20 years younger than his "coachee." He did NOT tell my father what to do. Instead, Reverend McNeil used an approach that helped my dad come to his own conclusions. He *acknowledged* (articulating a deep knowing of the client) Dad's integrity by noticing and remarking that he took his job as an elected public official very seriously. He praised my father for his stewardship of the faith that had been placed in him by the voters. The politician and the preacher forged a trusting, collaborative and active partnership.

Authentic political leaders listen deeply to their own inner voice and the voices of others before formulating different perspectives from which to choose.

Authentic leaders manage the paradox of being certain and confident in their own opinion while seeking, and reflecting on, the opinions of others. They are always open to questioning and learning about issues, and willing to allow new information to modify their opinions and decisions if appropriate. They are willing to "take a new picture" and see things differently. They are not afraid to admit that they don't know, that they struggle, or that they are sometimes wrong. Ultimately, however, they own their own beliefs and decisions.

Another coaching technique Reverend McNeil used was *reframing* (interpreting data in a different way). He pointed out that the Bible does not condemn drinking alcohol. Jesus himself drank wine. In fact, when the host of a wedding noticed that he was running low on wine, did he send someone out to the package store to buy more? Did he just explain that the guests would have to make do with water because of their earlier gluttonous consumption of wine? Did he say, "Hey, when you're out, you're out"? Did he condemn them for the sin of wine consumption? No. He simply asked Jesus for help. And Jesus contributed more wine. With that story, Reverend McNeil helped my father see another perspective from which to make his decision.

Another time that the minister helped others reframe and stood behind my father in the face of dissention was the day he went to Troyce Jackson's service station, where all the men gathered to discuss issues and sometimes to play checkers. The men were talking about the beer issue. One of them turned to Reverend McNeil and said, "A bunch of Baptists are going to Lawrenceville to talk against the sale of beer in the county. Are you going with them?"

Without cracking a smile, Reverend McNeil said, "No. The sale of beer in this county doesn't affect the Methodist congregation."

Someone else asked, " Really? Why not?"

"Because Methodists all drink hard liquor; they don't fool with beer," he replied. Everyone had a big laugh and the challenge was diffused. He stood strong for his client.

Authentic political leaders set goals based on values.

I was not part of the coaching conversation between the minister and my dad; however, I imagine that, somewhere in the meeting, they focused on goal-setting and intention. It might not have been explicit, because those terms weren't popular yet. The bottom-line question, explicit or not, however, would have been what mattered most. That would have been doing what was right for the future and taking the risk of not getting reelected. And yet, I am guessing that the two of them expressed the humanity of wanting to be loved, wanting to maintain friendships, wanting to please people. I picture them standing in the dilemmas of short-term vs. long-term, popular thing vs. right thing. When all is said and done, the most important goal is being of service to the real needs of the people.

In a recent interview with Reverend McNeil, I discovered that, to this day, he has never tasted an alcoholic beverage. He has personal convictions, and he makes his choices accordingly. However, J. B. McNeil did not try to influence the decision based on his own values. He held the client's agenda without making it his own.

Authentic political leaders have the courage of their convictions.

On March 13, 1961, all three commissioners voted to allow the sale of beer in the county—the first legal sale of alcoholic beverages in Gwinnett. In the late 1990s, Elliott Brack, a newspaper publisher for the Gwinnett County section of *The Atlanta Journal–Constitution* reflected on that time: "Indeed, the commissioners had turned beer into water for its 4,500 Gwinnett customers of those days."

Brack continued: "It took considerable political courage by Freeman, Elinburg and Corley to vote passage of the beer ordinance in the county. They caught the devil from many. And what happens in such situations? Yes, it was felt at the polls. These three commissioners were all replaced in the 1965 election. Yet their finding a way to save the county water system was the fuel, if you can think of water as fuel, for the explosive growth that Gwinnett County has seen ever since."

Think too of the impact on the county's reputation had the water system gone bankrupt. Gwinnett would have been tainted with this bankruptcy, perhaps being hurt even until today.

> *"The length of the term of office of a leader should not really matter that much. What is crucial is what a leader actually does while in office, in service to his people. The impact of such service can outlast a leader's term of office."*
> — Nelson Mandela
> *as quoted from a conversation with Professor Njabulo Ndebele*
> *University of Cape Town Vice-Chancellor*

Today, Gwinnett is one of America's fastest-growing counties, and has been for the past 20 years, and business is booming. Jobs are up, unemployment is down. More to the point, a second water filter plant opened in 2004 to meet Gwinnett's future drinking water needs.

Wastewater treatment capacity is also expanding with a 40-million-gallon-per-day addition to the water records center, a new pump station, upgrades at three smaller treatment facilities and 65 miles of new water mains.

I certainly could include the other two commissioners in my list of authentic political leaders. After all, they also made the courageous vote that served the county, yet cost them the election. Unfortunately, however, I don't know about their internal journey. I *witnessed* my father's decision making.

Authentic political leaders never stop searching and learning and growing.

Now let's fast-forward to 2007. I am taking off my daughter lens – as best I can – and putting on my coaching lens. In the political arena, this change of glasses symbolizes the difference between a staffer or campaign manager and a coach. The first category is like Betsy, the daughter. I was loyal, and I had skin in the game. I was close to the action, so there was no way I could have been objective about how Dad made his decision. If I could have signed a paper to get him out of the line of fire, I would have. There were certainly things I wanted him to say and do that would have been born of *my* emotions and thoughts, not his. Being an elected official puts people in difficult circumstances. It's not all about ribbon-cutting and baby-kissing and photo ops. It's scary out there.

How does one, in the words of Rudyard Kipling, *keep your head when all about you are losing theirs and blaming it on you…trust yourself when all men doubt you?* One answer is to create a structure that increases the likelihood of that reality.

Let's put the spotlight on the role that my coach example, Reverend J. B. McNeil, played. One definition of coaching is: A powerful alliance designed to forward and enhance the lifelong process of human learning, effectiveness and fulfillment. (*Coactive Coaching*)

In *The Wounded Healer*, Henri J. M. Nouwen writes:

Perhaps the main task of a minister is to prevent people from suffering for the wrong reasons. Many people suffer because of the false supposition on which they have based their lives. That supposition is that there should be no fear or loneliness, no confusion or doubt. But these sufferings can only be dealt with creatively when they are understood as wounds integral to the human condition. Therefore, ministry is a very confronting service.

I don't mean to suggest that coaches are synonymous with ministers (although Dad's minister was certainly a helpful coach). Coaches are not called to prevent anything. The client is in charge. I do believe that one task of the coach is to facilitate the translation of "shoulds" into "choices," while accepting the person right where they are. Coaching can also be a confronting service that requires mutual accountability. Successful coaching relationships require that the participants cocreate how they work together.

Now, looking through my daughter's lens again, I believe that my father, perhaps after more agonizing, might have made the call he made with or without his coach, but he would not have learned as much as he did about himself and how his values affected his public service. His favorite saying was, "The only real trouble I have ever had in my life is with me, myself and Minor." I think Reverend McNeil was a player in helping Dad reach into the magnificence of "he, himself and Minor." And Minor Morton Corley stepped into a picture of authentic, courageous political leadership.

Authentic political leaders create inspiration that endures over time.

My dad passed away in 1991, and yet, to this day, when I run into people who knew him, they tell me of their deep respect. They remember him as one who acted out of his own spiritual center as an authentic leader in home, community, church, job and public service in ways that helped others come to a realization of their God-given abilities and talents. Of course his inspiration will always live within me. I was lucky enough to witness his joy in serving, as well as his struggles to make wise—and sometimes unpopular—decisions for the good of the people he served.

Retelling this story awakens my deep desire to witness more of today's political leaders following my father's example. Members of Congress, state leaders and other politicians work hard on creating a positive image, so we usually know little about them that they don't want us to know.

I want to hear more about their struggles. I want to know that they will stand up for their beliefs. I want to know that they have my real needs in mind as they make decisions. I want to hear less about the other guy's mistakes, shortcomings and flaws, and more about the leader's own perspectives and how they arrived at them. I want to be inspired by their courage and insatiable thirst for learning. I want them to make citizens (like me) better for the world and the world better for its citizens.

Such leaders exist. I know some of them. You, the reader, may be such a leader. If so, I salute you. These authentic leaders accept that leadership begins within. They know there is strength in struggling for answers, and they spend time in contemplation and in conversation with others to make sure they have the full range of leadership behaviors at their disposal. They are the ones who make the dream of "a civic society carried to its utmost" possible. They internalize the words of the poem on the next page: "If" by Rudyard Kipling.

If

Rudyard Kipling

If you can keep your head when all about you
Are losing theirs and blaming it on you;
If you can trust yourself when all men doubt you,
But make allowance for their doubting too;
If you can wait and not be tired by waiting,
Or being lied about, don't deal in lies,
Or being hated, don't give way to hating,
And yet don't look too good, nor talk too wise.
If you can dream—and not make dreams your master;
If you can think—and not make thoughts your aim;
If you can meet with Triumph and Disaster
And treat those two imposters just the same;
If you can bear to hear the truth you've spoken
Twisted by knaves to make a trap for fools,
Or watch the things you gave your life to, broken,
And stoop and build 'em up with worn-out tools;
If you can make one heap of all your winnings
And risk it on one turn of pitch-and-toss,
And lose, and start again at your beginnings
And never breathe a word about your loss;
If you can force your heart and nerve and sinew
To serve your turn long after they are gone,
And so hold on when there is nothing in you
Except the will which says to them: "Hold on!"
If you can talk with crowds and keep your virtue,
Or walk with kings—nor lose the common touch,
If neither foes nor loving friends can hurt you,
If all men count with you, but none too much;
If you can fill the unforgiving minute
With sixty seconds' worth of distance run—
Yours is the Earth and everything that's in it,
And, what's more, you'll be a man, my son.

Apply the Insight
Four Questions to Answer

- What passionate belief would cause me to stand firm before great powers – even though my knees are shaking?
- How do I separate the REAL needs of the people I serve from their presenting needs and wants?
- Whom do I trust without reservation? What criteria do I use to make that critical decision?
- What are the lasting contributions I am making through my political service?

Betsy Corley Pickren, M.Ed., PCC, CPCC
Facilitated Learning, Inc.
Duluth, Georgia
770.263.7736
betsy@facilitatedlearninginc.com

Betsy Corley Pickren is president of Facilitated Learning, Inc., which focuses on promoting healthy, vibrant leaders and teams in organizations. Clients include: Turner Broadcasting, Cox Communications, the State Merit System of Georgia, the US Department of Agriculture, Emory University Libraries and CompuCredit. Betsy has a special interest in supporting people in elected public office to lead with authenticity, integrity and courage.

From 1982 to 1995, Betsy was an associate with Zenger-Miller, one of the nation's largest leadership development firms, where she trained facilitators in Fortune 100 companies, government agencies and international organizations. As vice president for Client Services, Betsy's segment of the company served the needs of more than 3,000 clients. Betsy also has firsthand experience on the "client side" through in-house management positions in banking and government. She was a member of the Carter-Mondale Transition Team and later was supervisor of Presidential personnel for The White House.

Betsy began her career as a high school teacher in Gwinnett County, Georgia, where she was named "Star Teacher." Her interest in the continued vitality of political leadership can be attributed to the fact that both her father and grandfather served as county commissioners.

She has been active in a variety of community and professional organizations. A mentor for PathBuilders (a mentoring program for women leaders in business), she has also served as past president of the Georgia Coach Association and co-chair for the first annual Atlanta PRISM Awards, which celebrate excellence in coaching in organizations.

Betsy earned a master's degree in Adult Education Program Management from Georgia State University. She is certified by the Coaches Training Institute, and credentialed as a Professional Certified Coach through the International Coach Federation.

Winning the Power Play

Michelle Randall

If you want to test a man's character, give him power.
— Abraham Lincoln

Power is your important currency and also the greatest threat to your career. Power is having control, authority or influence over others, and yourself as well, especially in the form of appropriate restraint. It's critical to make the distinction between positional power and personal power. *Positional* power is the authority, control and even physical strength granted to you by a majority of votes or a political appointment. Unfortunately, it's fickle and fleeting; you have positional power only as long as you have the position. *Personal* power is cultivated and nurtured over a lifetime of learning, and you can rely on it to further your career and fulfillment because it is lasting.

Much has been written about how to gather, consolidate and wield *positional* power, but only a few politicians understand that coaching is used by many leaders, in all environments, to help cultivate personal power. I believe that developing your *personal* power allows you to use your influence effectively and avoid the seductive dangers of positional power at the same time.

Start by considering the career of a political leader I'll call Doug Robertson.

In college, Doug was an outstanding student and a fiercely competitive athlete. When he entered politics by running for the council of a large city, he felt like he was testing himself in the most competitive of professional arenas. Once in office, Doug was highly competent and gained notoriety as an aggressive risk-taker who acted quickly on his impulses. He often ridiculed colleagues' requests to reconsider an issue, joking that introspection was a weakness and antithetical to success.

Doug liked to push the limits of conventional thinking. In fact, his motto was "Act first and ask permission later." He quickly reached the state assembly with a reputation for being resourceful, enterprising and willing to test limits to make it to the next level of performance and attainment.

During his meteoric rise to success, Doug made huge sacrifices. His daughter was born while he was flying home from a campaign fundraiser. His professional successes came at the cost of missed dance recitals, forgotten birthdays and broken promises to his family. By the time he ran for Congress, the only time he and his wife were in contact was at joint campaign appearances. To meet the demands of his busy schedule, Doug often accepted the use of a private plane belonging to a local defense contractor. When he could get away, he went on work-related trips with lobbyists. Doug felt entitled to these luxuries of office because he had certainly sacrificed enough in serving the public good. His staff became like family, and Doug demanded loyalty—even going as far as dismissing longtime staff when he perceived them as being critical of some of his decisions.

After a few years of service at the national level, the majority party in Doug's state shifted, and he learned through the grapevine that his district was going to be redrawn in such a way that he would have a very tight race to keep his seat. Doug was furious and his competitive instincts were at their height. This was *his* district, and he wasn't about to let it slip away from him! He started talking with senators in the new majority party about ways he could get a better index, and began funneling some of his PAC money into state coffers. He achieved the better index and his reelection looked safe … until the deal he had made became public.

Doug was surprised by the furor his bargain had set off. While he had expected that his party and his constituents would be pleased that he would keep his seat, he was wholly unprepared for what he considered their overreaction at the way he had assured it. As media scrutiny increased, the private plane and lobbyist-funded trips came to light. Doug became a poster child for corruption and something of a national joke. He was trounced in his election race, which effectively ended his career in public service. Even several years later, he was still trying to comprehend how the tide turned so dramatically.

Stories like Doug's illustrate what I've come to call "winning the game while losing yourself." It's a familiar scenario wherein ambitious, highly intelligent, hard-driving people follow years of swift and steady ascent with career-crippling misperceptions and failures in judgment.

Having a winning relationship with power without losing yourself is a delicate needle to thread that requires deliberateness and vigilance. There's something about the pursuit of power in highly-competitive environments that reshuffles the inherent makeup of individuals. The contents of a person's character remain the same, but the relative importance of key characteristics changes. This often means that some emotional intelligence attributes and values that were key in achieving power (such as perceptiveness, empathy, restraint and a commitment to serving the public) are relegated to a minor role, while other inherent attributes (such as competitiveness, justification and ego) take over in a way that compromises the person's ability to achieve their vision. In Doug's case, when his personal value of winning took over, he compromised his professional ethics without reflection and with notional justification. He also misjudged his importance to his party and constituents, which came from his inappropriate feeling of ownership toward his position.

But why would someone who had shown outstanding perception and political ability become prey to such disastrous misperceptions? It is common that the more leaders insulate themselves with loyalists who do not, or cannot, speak the hard truth, the farther they retreat into their own lonely reality instead of the reality of the people they are serving. What Doug failed to do was cultivate his personal power by creating a forum for self-reflection and professional development that matched his ever-increasing professional power. He also failed to seek out external individuals, like coaches, who would be so committed to his success that they would hold up a mirror for him to face. Raw truth would certainly have been hard for Doug to engage, but his political career depended on him facing reality.

Finally, while Doug prepared himself to attain steadily expanding positional power with his career rise, he failed to consider the effect it would have on his judgment, and he put nothing in place to manage himself before being confronted with difficult decisions. Because he didn't cultivate personal power, his boundaries were weak which made decisions he made in the moment more dangerous.

Doug's story is where most minds go when hearing about a politician's poor relationship with power. However, there's another career-compromising phenomenon when politicians fail to prepare for power. Wielding power can at times be overwhelming, frightening and humbling—especially when we're uncertain of the ramifications of our choices. It causes some to shrink back and not play full out. To illustrate this, consider the career of Helen Booth.

Helen entered political life through community service and was well liked. When announcing his retirement, a local city council member encouraged Helen to run for his seat. She won easily and became a dependable moderate voice that could create harmony among council members. The council revolved the mayor's seat and, after Helen had served several years, it was about be her turn. However, shortly before Helen's turn, an aggressive, up-and-coming new member of the council recommended changing the revolving order in his favor.

Helen was disappointed, but she didn't pursue the issue because she feared looking egotistical, and she was actually a little bit relieved. Before Helen's next opportunity to become mayor, a former colleague who had become a county supervisor asked Helen to come work for her as assistant deputy chief of staff. Helen was excited about the potential of serving the community on a larger scale through this position. However, what Helen found was frustration. The very people she wanted so desperately to serve were abusing the system, and the county bureaucracy was slow-moving and inefficient. She turned to her staff to discuss her disappointment but, instead of crafting solutions, they ended up complaining and assigning blame. Helen took her problems home to her husband and soon exhausted his ear, which created upset at home. When her supervisor lost an election, Helen moved to the security of a county job, where she stayed until she took early retirement.

Helen's story gives us a view into losing the game by giving up both personal *and* professional power. She lacked the courage to claim the mayoral position she had earned, and justified it through inappropriate modesty. By doing so, she failed to acknowledge the influence she had been granted throughout her years of service. At the supervisor's office, Helen abdicated the authority of her role by succumbing to frustration and giving up her personal power through gossip with her staff.

One similarity that Helen and Doug shared is the inadequate external support to recognize their obstacles to success and to build a sustainable relationship with power. Both were relying on their staff, or people in their lives, who didn't have the capacity or boundaries to support them in the ways they needed. This is a common hazard; it is only the highly perceptive political leaders who catch this lack and turn to external sources for feedback.

I often support my clients in developing a plan for sustainable success with power. They use it to masterfully wield their professional and personal power for service to their stakeholders and for their personal fulfillment (not gratification). I believe that, despite their different paths, if Doug and Helen had considered their attitudes toward power in advance, their stories could have had different outcomes.

Winning Your Power Play

Here's much of what I walk my clients through to create their plans—something we *tellingly* call "winning the power play."

Take an Inventory

To start, we take an inventory of both the positional and personal power the client has at their fingertips. In ascertaining their positional power, we look at the control, authority and influence built into their position. Remembering the position is transitory—it's the "power suit" the client gets to wear for a certain number of years, not their identity. As one well-respected political leader told me, "My job is to be the best possible steward of this position. It doesn't belong to me."

Personal power, in contrast, is the one thing that truly belongs to us, and its cultivation is a lifelong challenge. Another leader stated it succinctly: "If I'm not moving forward, I'm moving backward." My clients and I inventory key areas, including emotional intelligence, personal responsibility and meaningful contribution. Sometimes we include interviews with the client's family, staff and selected colleagues. From these conversations, we can assess the client's *perceived* and *real* mastery of personal leadership, as well as consider whatever perception gaps are brought to light. We also use information from key stakeholders to identify areas of opportunity that are apparent to others but have remained unrecognized by the leaders themselves. After these evaluations, the client and I have a basis for creating a plan for them to use power—not the other way around—by cultivating their personal power and managing themselves with positional power.

To start drawing your road map, begin by recognizing all the power at your disposal:

1. Look at the control, influence and might you have over your stakeholders—including constituents, staff and family members.
2. Ask your stakeholders how they perceive your control, influence and strengths.

3. Consider the effect your words and actions are having on your stakeholders.
4. Recognize when you exercise restraint with power. Is it in service to others or to the process? Could it be coming from your own comfort, fear or false modesty?
5. Reflect on this process. What did you learn? How can you improve?

Connect with Your Vision

I assume you have a vision and/or a guiding principle for your public service. Make sure it is specific and keep it current. Routinely ask yourself:

- What does it looks like for me to win at the game of life?
- What values are fundamental to me?
- What would tempt me to betray my vision? And what exterior hindrances do I have in place to stop me from doing so?

A midwestern state representative recalls an exchange he witnessed between Rep. Paul Wellstone and then-President George H. W. Bush. Rep. Wellstone used the power of his office to question some of the President's actions, despite their meeting in an intimidating atmosphere. In recalling this story, the leader said that it taught him to connect with his vision daily because "you don't know when you'll find yourself in a moment that's key for being courageous in service of your vision. If the moment comes and you're not certain if you have it in you, you won't be prepared."

The most straightforward way to stay true to your vision is to avoid the temptations of the trappings of office and keep your life simple. As examples, both Jimmy Carter and Warren Buffett still live in the same houses they lived in before becoming President and Nobel Prize winner, and "the Oracle of Omaha," respectively.

Get Plenty of Honest and Agenda-Free Feedback

Surround yourself with believers who will regularly infuse life into your passion for your vision, and who can get you to smile at the end of a really tough day. Make sure you have, among those cheerleaders and champions, an assortment of courageous and insightful people, like a coach, who care enough to call you out, who challenge your thinking and speak any hard truths that others, including you, may be stepping over.

One of the keys used by leaders who are successful in navigating the impact of power is the careful selection of the characteristics of the people they keep closest to them. It's this resource of honest responses and reactions that helps compensate for self-reflection lost to demanding schedules and our simple human inability to see ourselves fully all the time.

Evaluate:
- How many people do you regularly speak with who have no agenda for you?
- When was the last time you received eye-opening feedback about your performance?
- To whom do you confide your fears?

Prepare for Colliding Values and Professional Ethics

Knowing your vision and being grounded in your values aren't enough to protect you alone. The most corrupt political leaders became that way by abusing the power of their position in service of their vision and values. Your values guide your choices and behavior, and while they may have a lot in common with the ethics of your profession, the many nuances of values can cause them to conflict.

To illustrate, let's play with the value of service, a cornerstone of political leadership. Imagine that your area were plagued by abnormally high, and rising, instances of children's leukemia. If you became privy to classified information that the local water supply contained carcinogens being leaked from a secret weapons facility, would you tell your constituents to stop drinking the water? Even if it compromised the secrecy of the weapons facility?

While this scenario seems like the stuff of fiction, exercises such as these are worthwhile in testing your limits as you prepare for far more subtle, incremental conflicts. Consider:

- In what events would you be willing to bend, even break, the rules?
- What could you put into place to slow down the process of stepping over the line to give yourself time to think and choose wisely?
- What justifications do you think you would use to break the rules? Know what you would say to yourself so you can recognize it and catch yourself as it is happening.

Work the Plan

Working the plan won't happen by accident. You need to make time to reflect and ground yourself every day, especially on those days that seem too chaotic to do so. Even without having a Blackberry constantly interrupting him, Leonardo da Vinci said, "Every now and then, go away and have a little relaxation. To remain constantly at work will diminish your judgment." You don't have to take a major vacation for relaxation—even small daily increments that add up to a couple of hours a week can be enough to invest in your most valuable asset: yourself.

Create accountability by communicating your plan in depth and detail, especially to those people who will speak the hard truths. Ask them to hold you accountable, and when they do, don't justify your actions, instead hold your response to the words "Thank you." You will learn more when you force yourself to listen.

Look for ways to develop structural accountability. My dual roles as business owner and mother are an example: I love working with my clients and I love being with my children, so I corral my workaholic tendencies by working three days a week. My kids are only enrolled in daycare for those three days. If I want to add a day of work, the daycare fee is stiff, and that's when they have space for both kids. The hassle creates structural accountability that throw a tallow flag that make me chose thoughtfully. In which areas could you use extra help in being accountable? To rein you in, consider creating something structural outside of yourself.

When I talk with emerging political leaders about plans for making the right choices with power, I often get the same response: They assure me that they have the compass inside them. Some resist the genuinely hard work I've outlined for making that compass explicit. I've even heard the justification that they have to win first for it to be a consideration. However, once they win, their schedules are full and they protest that they have enough to do without creating "extra" time to receive external feedback or pursue personal and professional development. Those are usually the same ones who can't possibly conceive of their relationship with power ending in failure. Which means, for some of them, it will.

Apply the Insight
The Power to Please

One of the most powerful political leaders around once told me, "A big part of my job is listening with compassion and still saying No." As difficult as this is, it can be even more challenging in your personal life, because the mandate can get murky and the tug on the heartstrings can be greater. Here's a simple five-step process for decisions that foster lasting relationships:

1. **Choose, don't react.** Create a minute to think, even in a social situation.
2. **Look through three sets of eyes.** Think about the stakeholders in your life who will be affected (your family, for instance). Then think about how your decision will affect the requestor.
3. **Consider next, next, next.** What will the impact be on your stakeholders *next* week, *next* month and *next* decade?
4. **Choose yes, no, or renegotiate.** Remember that you can always renegotiate for a better solution!
5. **Respond for the future.** People treat us the way we train them. The way you respond to the request will influence the quality and frequency of future requests. Let people know how to please you—don't make them guess!

Michelle Randall, MBA, PCC, CPCC
Glass Houses Coaching & Consulting, Inc.
Morgan Hill, California
866.517.7291
michelle@glasshousescoaching.com

Michelle Randall is CEO of Glass Houses Coaching & Consulting, Inc., which serves people in the public eye. Their clientele includes political leaders, celebrities, sports figures, business executives, and their families and staff. Services include executive coaching and management consulting to help prominent people to identify and express their legendary leadership.

Prior to cofounding the company, Michelle was the principal and lead executive coach for The Juncture Company, which specialized in leadership development and corporate training. Michelle has worked as an executive in both the high-tech and construction industries, where her specialty was new market development. In high-tech, she ran the marketing function and launched both a company and its innovative product. Michelle was a pioneer in sustainable business, introducing the first green-building product line at a mainstream supplier. She went on to serve in the novel position of director of sustainability, encompassing values-based leadership of marketing, finance and operational activities.

Michelle's experience spans the globe, from working with CEOs from Asia, Africa, Europe and the US, to sharing black-market vodka with young leaders of change in the Soviet Union. She lived in Germany for years, and for part of that time managed international business contacts for the CEO and vice president international at Deutsche Telecom, the world's third largest telecommunications company. Michelle earned a Master of Business Administration at the Monterey Institute of International Studies, and a Bachelor of Arts from Eleanor Roosevelt College at the University of California, San Diego. She is a graduate of the Coaches Training Institute, a Professional Certified Coach, and a member of the International Coach Federation.

You Are a Visionary

Heather Cummings Jensen

It's an honor to introduce to you executive coaching, a tool we think is as beneficial as democracy itself, and one you'll want to take advantage of because you're a visionary. I know you are because you have picked up this book. My hunch is that you're looking for something that will help you get closer to achieving your dreams for public service and curious about how coaching can get you where you want to be.

What else do I know about you? I know that, as a visionary, you see possibilities and opportunities where others do not. You are looking not just for a "process improvement," as they say in the corporate world; you want a breakthrough.

You're able to see strategic opportunities and match new ways of doing things with those opportunities. Whether you're running for office, you're an elected office now, you belong to party leadership, or you're in a political capacity of another sort, you have a dream, and you're more committed to that dream than to doing things the way they have always been done.

You're a visionary because you know that, at this time in history, something more is needed in public service. You can feel it—sense it—in your bones. You may be very clear about what's needed, have your ideas fully formulated, and have begun engaging partners in your vision. Or you may have just an inkling that something more is needed in our society.

You likely have been fascinated by how Republicans began using language over thirty years ago to shift and shape their message, employing more visceral language like "death tax" rather than "estate tax" to further their objective of decreasing taxes. Whether you agree or disagree with this approach, there's a part of you that is intrigued by the innovation.

You want to be an innovator too. So, regardless of your party affiliation, you find yourself a little disappointed that Democrats are now organizing themselves to do the same thing Republicans did by shaping their message through the words they use. You want to see a quantum leap, not just a replication of the things that have worked for others. You want to lead in a way that goes beyond spinning words and gets to the heart of public service.

But you may be a bit tentative. You may never have entertained the idea that you are a visionary. To be a visionary may seem like you need someone else to bestow the title. But modesty does not serve you or your country. The evolution of our democracy and political system requires that you step forward and offer your leadership in accordance with the vision you have.

You may still think that the urges you have, the rumblings in your belly, the whispers in your ears are just things that you imagine—they don't mean anything. In coaching, we call that pesky doubting voice that starts talking in your head at inopportune times the "gremlin." The gremlin loves to ask the question, "who are YOU to think you could make a difference?"

Marianne Williamson offers the best response to the gremlin when she writes in *A Return to Love*:

> Our deepest fear is not that we are inadequate. Our deepest fear is that we are powerful beyond measure. It is our light, not our darkness, that most frightens us. We ask ourselves, *Who am I to be brilliant, gorgeous, talented, fabulous?* Actually, who are you not to be? You are a child of God. Your playing small doesn't serve the world. There's nothing enlightened about shrinking so that other people won't feel insecure around you. We are all meant to shine, as children do. We were born to make manifest the glory of God

that is within us. It's not just in some of us; it's in everyone. And as we let our own light shine, we subconsciously give other people permission to do the same. As we're liberated from our own fear, our presence automatically liberates others.

Why Do We Need Visionary Leaders at this Time in History?

Let's step back for a minute and look at the evolution of politics and some of the dynamics of our society that may be inspiring you to seek "something more" for modern democracy.

In her book, *The Politics of Hope,* Donna Zajonc adapted the stages of community and spiritual and human development, using the work of Elisabeth Kubler-Ross, M. Scott Peck, Erik Erikson, Robert Kagan, Ken Wilber, Stephen Covey, Don Beck, other anthropological researchers and philosophers, and her 30 years of experience in politics, to help us understand what she calls the *Four Stages of Political Evolution*:

1. **Anarchy**
2. **Traditionalism**
3. **Resignation**
4. **Conscious public leadership**

Each of these phases, just like the stages of evolution into adulthood, are valuable and needed. You can't easily move to one stage without first experiencing the one before. The opportunity lies in recognizing that they are simply stages of evolution. The power lies in knowing when it's time to move forward and to provide the vision for what's next.

	Stage 1	Stage 2	Stage 3	Stage 4
	Anarchy	**Traditionalism**	**Resignation**	**Politics of Hope**
Political Point of View	"All authority, political or otherwise, is inherently evil."	"We must defeat the opposing party to do good."	"Politics is irrelevant to our lives."	"Politics is a vehicle to create alliances with others for the common good."
Level of Hope	"There is no hope. Destroy the system."	"Winning is our only hope."	"Politics is hopeless. We must create an oasis/shelter in private life."	"Where there is integrity, there is hope."
Political Action	Reactive, rebellious.	Competitive, dominating, hierarchical; us vs. them	Neutral, disengaged.	Collaborative, inspirational.
Emotional Drive	Anger.	Fear, desire to win control.	Resignation, depression.	Love, respect, trust in goodness.
Trust	"Trust no one."	"Trust our candidate to solve our problems."	"Trust only yourself and your immediate family and community."	"Trust the evolutionary process and our collective wisdom to create fair policy."
Service	Serves self alone.	Appearance of selfless service masks service of personal ego.	Serves family and local community.	True selfless service based on addressing the needs of "seven generations" hence.
Motives	Destroy/ disempower government.	Elect a leader who will avert chaos and fix our problems.	Preserve values outside politics, acting within local community.	Consciously accept role of leadership as a contribution and a calling.
Power	Power against others at any cost; Lose/Lose.	Power over others; Win/Lose.	Personal power within a limited framework.	Power with others; Win/Win.
Truth/ Communication	"Truth is relative." (Believe no one.)	"The public can't handle the truth." (Information must be spun or withheld.)	"Truth is rare." (Corporate media is corrupted by political spin.)	"Truth is the essential nature of every human being."

The Four Stages of Political Evolution

Using the American example, Zajonc notes that an estimated 40% of American adults—50 million, both Republican and Democrat—are languishing in the state of Resignation around politics. They have given up because they see a society stuck in a Traditionalism mode of operation, "one built upon polarized parties, inauthentic—power politics, favors for the few, mediocre actions based on short-term thinking, fearful attacks, and a pervading distrust." So that evolution toward what is next can continue, Zajonc urges us to accept that the current form of our democracy no longer works for our needs.

It is this resignation in the public's hearts and minds that you, as a visionary leader, are tapping into, and it is time for you to take us to this next stage—out of Resignation and into Politics of Hope.

Acting on Your Visions

While you may have a sense of what's needed to get us to Politics of Hope, you may enjoy dreaming about new ideas more than putting them into action. While dreaming is one strength of a visionary, our political systems need the insight and the possibilities you see to be put into action.

Another obstacle to making your visions real can be the inability to put your ideas into words so others can understand them. This can be frustrating, because people may not "get" what is so clear in your mind— what you can see without having to explain the link between ideas—and you may have a hard time delegating some of the more routine elements of putting your vision in action.

This is an area in which a coach can be helpful. Your coach can be a sounding board who appreciates what you see and who wants to know and understand more. They will ask you questions when an idea isn't clear and help you continue to shape the ideas you may not yet have had the chance to speak out loud.

While I can't coach you on paper as I would by phone, I do invite you to consider these questions for the sake of articulating your visions:

- Imagine that you are speaking to someone with a different background, and use simple language to express what you are thinking. As you describe your idea to them, enroll them in its appeal.
- Imagine that your idea was implemented 20 years ago. How would you describe the impact it has had on politics?
- As you listen to what's happening in the world, what are you longing to see take shape?

Answering the Call

At some point, you may feel pulled to act on your visions even when they are not fully formed.

To coaches Virginia Kellogg and Kathy Kuser, in their CLAIMS Model of Change, answering the call is a key step in the change process.

To answer the call is like saying a big Yes to something that you really don't understand, because callings are rarely clear and seldom come with a map that your mind can easily follow. That's what's so special about callings. They come to us from a much deeper place than our heads. For some, a calling is something they are compelled to do without much reasoning. For others, callings only make sense after being followed for a number of years when, with the perspective of time, the callee can see how they have been preparing to do this work all their lives.

Answering a call can require stepping through some fire, especially when it involves changing the status quo. This can be disconcerting to leaders, if they are not clear about the path they are taking; the process can feel like a spiritual quest or a choice we must make to be an instrument through which our life is played.

My coach once suggested that there is a collective mind out there and that, when we are tapped on the shoulder with an idea, it's ours to run with. If we don't, the idea will move on to someone else. It can be a bit surprising, just like in the game of Duck-Duck-Goose, when you realize that you're the one who's been tapped on the shoulder!

At the core of the political leadership process is being willing to accept and embrace change and to recognize that something new is emerging. While answering the call does have a spiritual element to it that can give us a sense that we must follow through, we always have the choice to pursue it or not.

This choice is what makes the experience powerful, whether we say Yes or No. With our decision comes a clarity of our intention and commitment for the next juncture of our lives.

If you decide to say Yes to the call to bring your visionary leadership to politics, you will move from sitting on the sidelines to being fully engaged in your life!

Take a moment now to consider these questions:

- Has anything shifted for you as you've read this chapter so far? If so, what?
- What could it be like for you to lead a political breakthrough of such magnitude that it will reverse public resignation and engage hope?
- What would it take for you to believe in yourself so much that you would consider acting on the call you feel for something different in politics?
- What breakthrough do you want to see and how can coaching be used to make it happen?
- What's the most painful, pressing political challenge you see and how can you use coaching to solve it?

Answering the Call Does Not Have To Be Hard

What's really fun about answering the call is that it's a lot easier to be fully engaged in your vision than it is to be on the sidelines in pain because you're frustrated, trying to figure things out, or being manipulated and controlled by doubts that are urging you to just play it safe and not make any waves! Phew, what a relief to simply answer the call.

Once you've made that step, you have what you need to move forward. You don't need advanced degrees, an additional assignment on a committee, or a chairmanship to be a leader in politics. Nor do you have to be born into the "right" family. You can use the knowledge and experience you already have.

You don't have to know all the details of how you are going to move forward, but you do need a willingness to experiment, to try something, to succeed or fail, and to learn for the next time. An executive coach can assist you by helping you learn from your successes and failures as you implement your vision and get back into action again.

Albert Einstein said, "The significant problems we have cannot be solved at the same level of thinking we were at when we created them." Executive coaches can help you think at new levels. I can hardly wait to see what emerges on the political landscape as a result of your leadership.

Apply the Insight

**Share your vision for a new political future with
10 colleagues, friends and constituents.**

Heather Cummings Jensen, CPCC
Conscious Politics
Athens, Georgia
706.534.5023
heather@heathercummings.com

Heather Cummings' work as an executive coach is an outgrowth of her deeply held values and her caring for the world.

In 1993, she attended the World Conference on Human Rights and, as a delegate of Rights of Women, London, she contributed to the final NGO Declaration. Fascinated by international politics, Heather traveled on a train chartered by the Women's International League for Peace and Freedom that stopped in St. Petersburg, Kiev, Bucharest, Sofia, Istanbul, Odessa, Almaty and Beijing. At each stop, she met with local women leaders in business and politics. At this time—1995—it became clear to her that the world is connected and that the policies of the West have impact around the world and vice versa.

While she had profound interest and caring about international politics, she recognized that the best way she could serve was to help her country "take care of its own backyard." Still, she wasn't clear about how she would do that until she became a professional coach after a successful career in the corporate world.

Heather recognized that there is an emerging need in the American political system for a structure that supports leaders in reflecting on the issues at hand, assessing them in light of their values, and consciously deciding on the next steps for their political leadership. To provide this structure for those in public service, Heather shifted the focus of her coaching practice to working with political leaders. For this reason Heather co-founded Southern Truth and Reconciliation.

Heather graduated cum laude from Occidental College, Los Angeles, with a degree in women's studies and an emphasis in politics. Heather is accredited through the International Coach Federation and is certified by the Coaches Training Institute.

The Value of Coaching for Leaders in the Public Domain: A Case Study

Hélène Beauchemin

I have been referred to clients who were not entirely excited about the prospect of coaching. For one of these engagements, I was called in because someone recognized a leader who was becoming harmful to himself and the organization as a whole. The following story recounts a real situation (the names have been changed to protect the privacy of those involved). It offers a glimpse into the pitfalls leaders can face when transferring their abilities and past ways of acting into a new setting, and shows how a coach can help. In this particular case, there was the added benefit of restoring a healthy working environment in a small agency.

My first move as a coach is to build trust with the client. In the case of David Jones, I strove to ensure that my client felt he was being seen and accepted for who he was—not as a discipline case or someone who needed fixing. I went in with the stated objective of getting to know him, and understanding what it was about his way of dealing with people that was not working.

David Jones had been a capable and vocal social activist, an academic, a private consultant and a staff member in a minister's office. That last position is a partisan one, and the focus on loyalty and defending the elected leader can lead to a blurring of the lines between civility, ethical behaviour and the achievement of timely results. In recognition of David's great service to the party in power, he was appointed to an executive position within the government. He was suddenly taken from the role of engaged activist and thrust into the role of government executive, with a mandate for social change that was set by the Prime Minister. In his new position, the focus was on social policy change for a specific citizen group. David did not have any management skills, but he was driven by his desire to create meaningful change for a segment of society.

In the political world he had come from, short-term bursts of intense activity were the norm, sort of like sprinting. In the bureaucracy, the pace is more long-term, like a marathon. Bureaucrats are in for the long haul, and society needs that stabilizing influence so they don't fall into total chaos every time there is a change in government. To an activist, the government is the enemy of visible change. As a political attaché, David had witnessed the frustration of politicians who were elected on a specific platform and felt the intense pressure to get something done that would be their legacy. As people in that environment drove themselves and those around them very hard, tempers would flare and language could degenerate to locker-room level. Coming from this background, David drove himself and anyone in contact with him very hard. Eventually it reached the point that his staff could no longer take the pressure. They also lived in fear that he would "blow a gasket" on the floor of the office and they would have to call emergency crews to revive him.

Mediators dealing with the situation called me in as coach after the staff said they were on the verge of registering a harassment complaint against David. It was an ultimatum. This presented a bit of a challenge to the beginning of the coaching relationship.

I chose to hold our first meeting on a Saturday morning at David's favourite coffee shop, rather than at his office, where everyone would see us meeting. He was simultaneously defensive and devastated. He sincerely liked his staff and didn't understand how they could say those things about him. He also didn't understand why they would not embrace his way of seeing the world. After all, they had been working in a secluded organization with the previous manager—a 25-year career civil servant.

When I met David, he had been in his job for 18 months. By that time, he had become so frustrated with what he perceived as resistance to change and slowness of due process that he had begun to confuse power with force. He was using more and more force in his attempts to get his point across. David fought what he perceived as his staff's resistance, by reverting to the habits that had served him well before: his wit, his incendiary writing style and his voice. Throughout our conversation, he kept returning to one or two sentences from the mediation, asking, "How could they say that?" He kept reliving the painful parts and telling himself how wrong his staff was and how he cared for each of them. Eventually we found an opening to move forward.

I met each member of his staff individually and discovered that they also cared for him, but they could not deal with his conduct any longer. We agreed on some strategies to enable them to take a stand instead of being victimized when David's behaviour started getting out of hand.

Then I met with David and got him to take a good look at himself—to make the distinction between his motivation for action and the actions themselves. This was tricky because, once he acknowledged that his behaviour was hurting his staff, he moved into the blame game. Eventually we were able to progress from "I am a horrible person, I am bad" to "I am not a bad person, but my actions are hurtful to all." Before he came to this point, he was in intellectual denial, telling me that he didn't understand what I was getting at, occupying our time with his stories and anecdotes, and feeling very smug with his superior intelligence. My challenge was to find a way through his armour.

David was a big man—6 feet 4 inches tall and about 250 pounds. He was smart, and had a quick wit and a sharp writing style. As an academic, he had the ability to both teach and entertain his students. He had been a star, and he reverted to that role with me, intending to impress me with his knowledge, stories and savoir-faire to derail me from getting to the core of the issue. I knew I had to stop him without breaking our bond of trust. I began by saying that the story was a fine one and I would like to hear more, but at some other time. That didn't work well enough, so I had to go visual and visceral. One day I saw a newspaper cartoon about the

Incredible Hulk. I cut it out and showed it to David, telling him, "David, this is what your staff sees when you rant and rave." He went absolutely white. He was completely shocked; he'd never viewed himself that way. In his mind, he was just a little guy trying to get big things to happen in his country. This provided the break that allowed me to add, "You now exercise a position of authority. You are the boss. You have the power to make the lives of your staff miserable if you want to. You have power over their performance appraisals and their careers. Instead of acting like a leader, you are behaving more like this big green hulk." This was the real beginning of our coaching journey. And the Hulk cartoon certainly contributed to the ultimate change in him.

The other contributing moment came when I acknowledged his past experiences as a successful lobbyist and activist. I presented the image of David and Goliath. Little David the activist has only his slingshot and his voice to gain the attention of the great government monolith. That approach was appropriate in his past, but now he was a representative of the government. Screaming at his staff and figuratively throwing rocks in the gardens of his departmental colleagues was counter-productive and totally inappropriate.

His first reactions were shame and fear. He felt shame about how others saw him. He recognized that his tolerance for ambiguity was low, and he was fearful of falling into the same behavioural patterns that had been so destructive in the past. His first reaction was to stay at home and send out emails, limiting his personal interactions with people. At first I supported this strategy, because everyone in the office was still emotionally raw; they were walking on eggshells when dealing with him, and everyone, David included, needed some breathing space.

When I met with the staff individually again, they were starting to miss him and his leadership. They said his behaviour had improved, but they never saw him and felt he had given up on them. I asked them if they had said these things to him. They were stunned! "We should give him feedback?" We pursued this subject and explored why they would be ready to give negative feedback, but not positive. I pointed out that David, as a person, needed the positive response as much as anyone else.

They offered to give him positive feedback six months down the road at performance appraisal time. So I asked them, "How would that work for you—waiting six months for positive feedback?"

I was able to get his staff to see David as a human being who needed their support as he was changing and improving his behaviour. This was another coaching moment for me as I faced the resistance from a group that had become quite comfortable with expressing resentment. They weren't eager to move out of that stance, which had served them well up until then. Getting them to own up to this was another turning point in David's evolution to being a manager.

Next, I had to provide David with a crash course in the essentials of management. This was when my own four decades as a manager came into play. At that point, you might say I moved from pure coaching to consulting, mentoring and training. I worked closely with him to prepare for the annual two-day staff retreat. The staff was apprehensive about the meeting because it had been the scene of a big blow-out the previous year. We decided that David would open the meeting and acknowledge the behaviour issue—the proverbial elephant in the room—in specific terms, without being maudlin. Then he would give the role of chairing the meeting to a trusted collaborator and announce that his own function would be to take notes in the back of the room. This was a way to get him to stop interjecting (which he did as naturally as breathing), learn to listen, and play a different leadership role.

After the session, David told me that it was the most difficult thing he had ever done. We had removed him from his usual place on stage, and he realized that he had gained respect, rather than losing it, as he first feared.

This is a good point to clarify the distinction between process and content agenda. Getting David to take notes had not been part of my content agenda as a coach; it was only a part of the process that would allow him to become a better manager and leader, which was his ultimate agenda. Think of it this way: Swimming laps in a pool is not the swimmer's agenda; it is just part of the process—the daily practice of strengthening muscles and achieving mastery of the sport. The immediate agenda, focused on immediate concerns, is necessary to achieve the ultimate agenda. As David's coach, my task was to come up with designs, exercises and practices that would allow this to happen for him.

I found that a sailing metaphor worked well for him, because he felt he had to carry the world on his shoulders and bring about massive change in a short time. A long-distance passage by boat requires teamwork, since no one can stay awake 24 hours a day. When there is a crew on board, each member takes a shift at watch. During your watch, you are at the wheel, responsible for the safe passage of the ship. If problems arise, you can always ask for help. When your watch ends, you can sleep as someone else takes over. With this image in mind, I asked him to consider what he had accomplished so far on his watch. If it was reasonable to think that the agenda had moved as far as it could for the time being, then maybe it was time to hand it off to someone who could implement what he had developed. Considering that possibility, I asked him to think about what kind of leader and manager he would need to be for the next leg of the trip.

This image really struck home for him, and he eventually realized that he had accomplished a lot by creating new legislation. He was relieved to have the opportunity to stop battling for a while. Up to that point, he had only known one mode of operation: push, push, push. For the first time, he took a step back and realized that he and his team had given their best, and now it was time for implementation—a different mode of operating. It would still require a lot of persistence, but with more finesse than force. Force, used too often, loses its effectiveness.

Two things were heartbreaking about working with David. The first was the unnecessary pain he and his team experienced. If he had had a coach from the beginning, the crisis situation might have been avoided. A new category of coaching called "on boarding" recognizes that, when people move into new organizations or responsibilities that are a stretch for them, it is preferable to have a coach right from the beginning. The most enlightened corporations are doing this now, and we definitely need to bring this practice into the political realm, particularly as politicos are appointed to executive roles.

There is a second bittersweet part to this story. After the coaching program had officially ended, we agreed on a follow-up program. I would be on call and come in every quarter to assist David and his team as needed. On my last visit to the office, just before the Christmas holiday, the mood had changed: Most of the tension was gone, and there was a sense of forward movement for all. David then left for a well-deserved holiday. He died in his sleep, alone in a foreign hotel. It was bittersweet because the struggle had been so hard for this man—so much more demanding on him than anything his staff had felt. In a sense, he was at peace at last, his battles fought and won.

I felt a great sense of gratitude. Before David died, his staff had come to understand what he stood for and wanted to accomplish. Afterward, as testimonials poured in from across the country, they saw what he had been trying to achieve. They bought into his vision for change and vowed to implement it. For me, this was a great example of the power of coaching. When I coach one person and a change comes about, the ripple effect goes far beyond that individual. It positively affects his environment, family and organization.

Some would say of this story that it was meant to be. I see a lesson to be learned—one that my colleagues and I are conveying to government. There is an increasing tendency to bring people into the senior ranks from outside government. These are people who have made a name for themselves, who are chosen because they are perceived as successful. Unfortunately, the success rate in these situations is abysmal. The political and public sector environments are entirely different. This is like putting people into a different culture where norms are not written and language is obtuse, and then expecting them to shine.

I want it to be clear to the leaders in our political arena that there is coaching available to them. Successful people do not rely solely on their raw talent and determination to succeed. They employ a coach, or a succession of coaches, as they evolve.

The coaching relationship is less about feeling good than about growth and excellence. The effect the change will have on your environment is something else your coach will address. Where will you find support in your world? Where will you encounter resistance to the change? Whose interests or sense of well-being will be threatened? How will you cope with these shifts? Will you feel, at times, that your family or colleagues are withholding their support or understanding of what you are going through? Each of these questions will be considered and answered throughout the coaching process and resulting change.

Is there a role for coaches in a public policy environment? Yes. I can't think of a place where such change is more needed, or can be more beneficial to us all as citizens. We deserve well-grounded and reflective political leaders, and they deserve nothing less from us than our expectations that they will meet these standards.

Apply the Insight —The 4-Second, 4-Step Practice

1. Release a deep out-breath and follow your breath with your mind as you exhale.

2. With your mind's eye, check where the tension lies in your body. When you have found it, relax that part (neck, shoulders, jaw). Relax discreetly—just a little bit, no need for large movements.

3. Whether you are sitting or standing, ensure that you are feeling centered and grounded (as if you might need to keep or regain your balance quickly).

4. Declare your intention to develop a quality you are presently working on. For instance: "What if I was just a bit more calm, or a better listener, or took the initiative, or refused to compromise on a core value, what would it look like?" Wait to see if anything comes up. If it does, trust your guts; if nothing comes up, keep on your present course. Repeat 20-30 times a day. Do this when you wake up, take a shower, eat breakfast, go to a meeting and drive (stop signs, red lights and elevator rides are great opportunities to practice).

Suggested reading:
The Life We Are Given by George Leonard and Michael Murphy
Mastery by George Leonard
The Intuitive Body by Wendy Palmer

Hélène Beauchemin, PCC
HKBP, Inc.
Ottawa, Canada
613.236.4847
helene@hkbp.ca

Hélène Beauchemin is president of HKBP, Inc., a management consulting firm for senior leaders seeking executive coaching and professional and personal development. She is a professionally certified integral coach trained at New Ventures West in San Francisco.

Because she has worked at senior levels in government, Hélène has the gift of demystifying leadership. Having spent many years working with provincial and federal governments in positions including assistant deputy minister, she is able to offer her clients coaching from her wealth of experience. She shows parliamentarians, seasoned executives, board members and association executives the best practices for being a leader people will want to follow and work for.

Executives at all levels need to enhance their skills and learn to read and understand a new environment. They turn to Hélène for help in honing these skills because they know she's lived it. "I've moved 36 times in my life; I've learned to quickly read an environment and culture."

She now resides in Ottawa, Ontario, Canada. She and husband Peter have a reconstituted family of two sons, three daughters and a dozen grandchildren, as well as a classic wooden motor cruiser that is their cottage on the water.

Inspired Leadership:
Knowing and Owning Your Core Values

Erika Gabaldon

As a public servant in America today, you have the power to direct the future of your communities and your country. What you do as a political leader makes a significant difference. You can help make the future better than the past; you can turn the present into a time for productive change. If you know and own what you truly value, you can tap into a deep reservoir of power that will sustain and inspire you as you work to build a better world.

My work as an executive coach permits me to observe how our daily values reflect our innermost selves. Those daily values are rooted in a few essential principles that guide how we think and act. I refer to these principles as "core values". Core values are innately positive: They connect us to our fundamental humanity and spring from the intrinsic good within all of us. As a public servant, you have the chance to more fully embrace the values that urge you to lead, and call you to serve, others.

This chapter will cultivate a deeper knowledge about values—a knowledge that hearkens to more than moral conduct or virtuous action—so that you can more intimately know what your values are and what they mean to you. I will share with you how knowing and owning your core values prepares you to turn political vision into potent, creative action. The conscious use of your core values allows you to inspire others, to generously stand up for what you believe in, and to powerfully influence the communities around you.

The Conscious Use of Core Values

Calculating risk is an everyday part of a public servant's life, and modern history is filled with examples of inspired leaders who weighed political risks against core values and chose to influence significant events of their time.

In 1950, Senator Margaret Chase Smith read her "Declaration of Conscience" to the Senate, denouncing Joe McCarthy for his anti-Communist tactics. She was the first US senator to speak out against McCarthy. Smith knew that her statements posed a risk to her political reputation, but she had a firm "creed" to rely on: "… Public service must be more than doing a job efficiently and honestly. It must be a complete dedication to the people and to the nation, with full recognition that every human being is entitled to courtesy and consideration, that constructive criticism is not only to be expected but sought, that smears are not only to be expected but fought, that honor is to be earned [and] not bought."

In 1967, Dr. Martin Luther King also risked his credibility as the leader of the Civil Rights Movement to make public his opposition to the war in Vietnam. King addressed clergy and laymen at the Riverside Church in New York City. He spoke to those who asked, "Why are you speaking about the war, Dr. King? Why are you joining the voices of dissent? Aren't you hurting the cause of your people?"

King was "saddened," but not swayed, by the doubts so many expressed, by those who proclaimed that peace and civil rights don't mix. In fact, his "calling" propelled his political direction. "For those who ask the question, 'Aren't you a Civil Rights leader?' and thereby mean to exclude me from the movement for peace, I have this further answer. In 1957, when a group of us formed the Southern Christian Leadership Conference, we chose as our motto: 'To save the soul of America.'…"

Both Smith and King spoke out—despite the potential risks—because their core values enjoined them to. Inspired, they had the courage to say what they felt was needed, no matter how unpopular their words were at the time. President Franklin Roosevelt met "fear" with determined action—and inspired Americans to shift their attention away from economic collapse and toward putting people back to work. Even President Dwight Eisenhower, a former Army general, demonstrated how he valued people more than the defense industry when he said, "Every gun that is made, every warship launched, every rocket fired, signifies in the final sense a theft from those who hunger and are not fed, those who are cold and not clothed."

Susan B. Anthony, Shirley Chisholm, Barbara Jordan, Bella Abzug and many others have defended better lives for women and demanded that "equality for all people" include women. Anthony made her relationship to her core values and to risk clear: "No matter what is done or not done, how you are criticized or misunderstood, or what efforts are made to block your path, remember that the only fear you need have is the fear of not standing by the thing you believe to be right. Take your stand and hold it; then let come what will and receive the blows like a good soldier."

These leaders shared one view despite their very different political alliances: In order to sustain themselves and inspire others, their political work had to emanate from their core values.

I've drawn from progressive examples within history for two reasons: (1) to exhibit how great leaders have purpose, passion and a willingness to act, and (2) to demonstrate that for willingness to become action, you need to know your core values and then let them guide you.

What are you committed to? Put that front and center in your political work so you know it—and everyone else does too. Then you can make conscious use of your core values whatever the risk or opportunity any political moment provides.

Know and Own Your Core Values

Public servants seek to better all communities—from local to global. They work hard, under laborious circumstances, to effect positive social change. While most political leaders carry strong hopes about what they'll achieve, some wind up lost in the political machinery. The political process can easily go awry, and massive bureaucracy or compromises can sidetrack the good work that many intend. That's why knowing your fundamental values is crucial; they join you to what you really care about, and they direct your political actions so you can be a catalyst for cultural change in the same tradition of King, Roosevelt, Eisenhower, Smith and Anthony.

A caveat: Knowing or owning your core values isn't a cure-all for the political difficulties you face. You won't be immune from pressure from others. You'll have emotional reactions that could be counter-productive, and you'll sometimes have to deal with your "shadow" side. But connecting with your core values provides a touchstone that you can refer to and rely on again and again. You'll be more aware of yourself and will have focus and direction that gives clarity and purpose to your political work. You'll have an intrinsic set of values that can guide all your actions, as well as a consistent identity that will endure regardless of cultural whimsy or the current political climate.

Connect with Your Core Values

Often people who run for office have a dream that guides them, but as elected officials, they can easily lose sight of this dream within the maze of political reality. Reconnecting with your core values is a powerful way to reinvigorate your dream and move it forward. There are many techniques for rekindling your core values. Here are a few:

- **Use a Process of Inquiry.** Your values reside within you, and a process of inquiry allows you to discover or reconnect with what's in your heart. Questions, asked by a coach or someone you trust, are a good way to get at what you care about. Deep questioning can reveal your values or intensify your connection to them and reaffirm your commitment to political work.

  Make use of questions designed to integrate the heart and mind. For instance, the answer to "What is important about the person you most admire?" will reveal much about your core values, showing you traits that you want to exhibit in your own life but haven't fully expressed. Also, using questions that take you inside another's experience will allow you to look more deeply inside yourself:

◊   What political leaders inspire you?
◊   What about their accomplishments motivate you?
◊   How have they handled themselves in difficult times?
◊   What qualities do you admire in them? How do they engender your respect?

The "wisdom" your heart conveys will help shape your political purpose and actions. The advantage of having an executive coach is that they can help you keep track of your values and will acknowledge when you're acting in alignment with them. You work hard and often deal with more defeats than victories, so your coach will also remind you that it's important to honor your victories. Claiming and celebrating them will help keep you inspired and motivated to persevere.

- **Explore Your Accomplishments.** Describe one of your greatest accomplishments. Look for what was most important about it for you. What you focus on may also reveal core values. For example, one of my coaching clients revealed that her greatest accomplishment was securing legislation for the building of a new community center. When she described the experience, she focused on the teamwork involved in getting the legislation passed. After further exploration, we realized that teamwork and collaboration were core values for her.

- **Let Your Imagination Speak.** Imagine yourself 10, 15 or 20 years from now, standing on a big stage with thousands of people in the audience. You are receiving an award for your political service. As you look back, what would you say your vision was? Your message? What did you accomplish? Hold that image of yourself but return to the present. Focus on leaders who have already had the kind of impact you want to have—Wangari Mathai, Cesar Chavez, Nelson Mandela. Would you like to be the next John F. Kennedy, Rosa Parks, Theodore Roosevelt? This is the kind of inspired—and inspiring—leader you can be when you know what truly motivates your actions.

Remember that your values are already a part of you. So, as you reflect on these questions, you are not making decisions about what you value—you are *discovering* or *reaffirming* what you value. Let what you learn guide you.

Apply the Insight
Reaffirm the Core Values of Your Political Work

Core values help you know, and move toward, what you want. They provide a foundation for inspired leaders to work from. Within your foundation is your higher purpose, your best intentions, the calling that brings you to political work.

- Reaffirm the core values of your political work by reflecting on the following questions:
- What brought you into politics?
- What do you want to accomplish more than anything else?
- What motivates your political work?
- What challenges do you need to overcome to achieve the political goals most important to you?
- How can your political actions and personal convictions work together?

Use Core Values as Fuel for Inspired Leadership

Your core values fuel you with:

Political Purpose

Core values bring together aspirations, higher purpose and experience. Two things result: (1) a political vision you can share with others and (2) your political purpose. What is the main reason you are in politics? What is most important for you to accomplish?

Sometimes you discover your political purpose, and sometimes your political purpose finds *you*. For example, when states began to secede from the Union, President Lincoln had to take a stand. He relied on his strong belief that all men are created equal to help him decide that slavery had to be abolished. "I have here stated my purpose according to my view of official duty; and I intend no modification of my oft-expressed *personal* wish that all men everywhere could be free." (Emphasis added)

Blueprint of Your Vision

Core values hold the "big picture." They keep you focused and on track while allowing you to do the step-by-step work to realize your overall vision. For example, Gandhi's commitment to nonviolence meant that he could not "hurt anything that lives," but it did not preclude his defying British laws that harmed Indian citizens. This blueprint—knowing what he could and could not do—propelled him to launch the Salt March, a 241-mile public protest against the expensive British tax on salt, an essential for India's poorest people. The success of the march strengthened Gandhi's leadership and pushed India's independence movement significantly forward.

Trust Account

Core values allow you to be consistent in word and deed. When you act with this congruency, people believe in you and deposit their trust into your account. Even when you must compromise, the few small checks you write against this trust account are not a threat to your strong balance, and they don't harm your long-term relationships with others. The minimal costs of doing business don't compromise the wealth of political good will you have accumulated.

In 2002, Minnesota Senator Paul Wellstone tapped into his trust account when, as the only Democratic senator up for reelection, he voted No on the Iraq Resolution, which would authorize President Bush to use force against Iraq with or without a United Nations mandate. Wellstone knew that 60% of his constituents supported military action against Iraq, but he held a deep belief that our country should make use of international cooperation and diplomacy before we decided on war. According to an October 3, 2002, article in the *Minneapolis Star Tribune*, Wellstone said this was a "life-or-death question for people" and added, "I'm not 38, I'm 58. And at this point in my life, I'm not making any decision that I don't believe in."

Colin McGinnis, a Wellstone staffer, later stated that Wellstone "really thought that if he voted against this [resolution], he might very well lose the race." Apparently, however, Minnesotans' trust in Wellstone was stronger than any disagreement they had with his vote. The day after he cast his vote, Minnesota election polls spiked in his favor.

Personal Style of Leadership

All political leaders have their own style, one that emanates from those ideas they are passionate about. Reflecting who you are allows others to connect with you. Knowing your core values allows you to define your leadership style and use it authentically. When you're authentic, others more easily like you—no matter how unique your style is. Ann Richards, former Texas governor, relied on humor and blunt honesty in both victorious and challenging times. Richard's style is exemplified in her 1988 Democratic Convention address. She said, "Twelve years ago, Barbara Jordan, another Texas woman, made the keynote address to this convention, and two women in 160 years is about par for the course. But, if you give us a chance, we can perform. After all, Ginger Rogers did everything Fred Astaire did. She just did it backward and in high heels."

The Stamina to Manifest Change

Your core values fuel you. They provide the essential nutrients you need to sustain your political vision day to day. The success you achieve by working from your core values is like muscle memory. You can draw on your positive experience again and again so that you have the stamina to persevere—no matter the conditions you must endure or the obstacles that get in your way. Shirley Chisholm said, "In the end, antiblack, antifemale, and all forms of discrimination are equivalent to the same thing—antihumanism. ... I am, was, and will always be a catalyst for change."

Core Values Bring Head and Heart Together

Good political decisions arise from the understanding of core values. These core virtues make you aware of what you know intellectually, as well as from your emotional and spiritual experience. They provide a framework for heart and head to work together in decision making. When a reporter asked Senator Wellstone if he was concerned about the negative political consequences he might face for having voted No to sending troops to Iraq, he answered, "I have to only do what my head and heart and soul tell me is the right thing to do. That's all I can do."

Your mind will assess all factors (political, economic, popular, special interest, etc.) that affect your actions, and logic will point you in a clear direction. If what's logical doesn't feel right to you, then you'll need to become more aware of what's in your heart as well as your head. Ask more questions and further explore the issues. Reflect on your feelings and experience. Look into your heart to remember what really matters to you.

You do not need to prefer the heart over the mind or vice versa. Knowing your core values allows you to discern and be responsive to what you think *and* what you feel. Minnesota representative John Lesch eloquently stated how inspired leaders allow their hearts and minds to work in tandem: "The miraculously and perennially victorious in this world are those who lead with their hearts. This is, of course, after sensible consultation with the head—but a hero's first step is always taken with a heart's whisper in his ear."

There may be times when you'll listen too much to your heart or your head, and you'll end up regretting your decision. If so, return to your core values and explore other possible decisions in light of those values. Use this knowledge in your next decision-making process. A beautiful example of this is found in the documentary, *One Bright Shining Moment*. In the film, Senator George McGovern states, "I regret my vote on the Gulf of Tonkin resolution more than any other vote I cast in 22 years of Congress. ... I still have reservations about it. I should have stayed with those reservations and voted No." Later however, McGovern, in alignment with his core values, not only stood up against the Vietnam War, but he built his campaign for the Presidency on withdrawing the United States from the war. McGovern was a strong catalyst for bringing the conflict to an end.

An Inspired Leader

Donna Zajonc, in *The Politics of Hope,* writes that elected public servants need to "govern in service to the collective good." This means that those you serve are not just your friends and neighbors, your constituency or the American people, but the global community and generations to come. Your core values are the compass that gives you political direction and points you toward service to others. Once you know your values, you can ask: Do my decisions honor my core values? Will my actions make use of my values? Do I act according to what I know my political purpose is? Am I acting with the heart of a servant? Do I benefit the collective good?

In March 2005, former President Bill Clinton spoke about his vision for a genuine global community. He measured every decision regarding his vision, no matter how simple or complex, against three questions: Does it promote shared responsibilities? Does it promote shared benefits? Does it promote shared values?

Your coach or a trusted colleague can help you develop similar questions that simply and consistently return you to what is essential in your work. They can remind you of the political directions you've chosen and help you progress steadily along your political path. As you identify and connect with your core values, you'll reclaim the heart of a servant, the essence of inspired leadership. You can ask: Do I inspire myself? Do my actions inspire others?

Owning your core values allows you to remain steadfast in your vision, and it gives you the courage to carry it out regardless of consequences or outcomes. The tremendous pressures, challenging issues and inherent problems within the political process don't have to be a threat to your political work. With your heart committed to service and core values you can rely on, you will advance your cause and lead with passion, integrity and honor. Your essential being and public self will align, and you'll be a leader for others in reliance, inspiration and vision.

Erika Gabaldon, MA, ACC
Glass Houses Coaching & Consulting, Inc.
Los Angeles, California
866.517.7291
erika@glasshousescoaching.com

Erika Gabaldon, president of Glass Houses Coaching & Consulting, Inc., serves people in the public eye, including political leaders, celebrities, sports figures, business executives, and clients' families and staffs. Credentialed through the International Coach Federation (ICF) and certified through Coach For Life, Erika offers life coaching and management consulting to help those who reside in the "glass houses" of public life to prepare, develop and thrive.

Erika is also trained as an Inspired Learning Facilitator through the Foundation for Inspired Learning (San Diego, CA) and holds a master's degree in Spiritual Psychology from the University of Santa Monica (Santa Monica, CA). She is a member of ICF (national and Los Angeles) and the Screen Actors Guild. She also serves on the advisory board of Young Progressive Majority (YPM), a social network of 20-30 year olds committed to increasing the vote for local progressive candidates and issues.

Erika is a true "democracy geek"; when she is not working, you'll find her reading books or articles on American politics, attending leadership conferences, or participating in political gatherings, activities and events.

Erika lives in Los Angeles with her husband, Spike Feresten.

Negotiating on the Same Side of the Table

Michelle Randall and Chad White

The "public process" is a series of negotiations among parties on the same side of the table. Any shared geography, regional or national boundary, or jurisdiction creates a de facto team. Facing the team from across the table are the challenges they both face at the time.

Unfortunately, this understanding of team unity gets lost in the face of ideological differences and competing agendas that individual members are advancing. These differences create team divisions that feel real but are, in fact, artificial. Members start to think that they are sitting across the table from each other, instead of on the same side, which can cause adversarial relationships to harden into partisanship. Too often the focus then becomes how to beat one another out of resources and power in pursuit of a triumphing agenda of personal self-interest. Even though the members are still on the same side of the table, they become antagonistic toward each other.

Imagine a basketball team split over passionate differences in strategy and refusing to work together, even taunting each other during a big game. This team would be stealing the ball from its own players, who would be blocking shots made by their own teammates, fouling and pushing each other out of bounds. In short, it would be a game of perplexing alliances or, even worse, a game of one-on-one-on-one-on-one. Would a team like this have a chance of winning a game? Most likely not. In fact, in a game with fractured teams scoring on their own teammates, how would you even determine the winner? Would fans (if there were any) buy tickets? Would they show up for the game? With this as a political reality, would voters actually show up at the polls? This seems like an absurd scenario, yet when unenlightened self-interest and partisan politics muscle their way through the political landscape, we often see the win being sacrificed.

All political leaders who share the same jurisdiction are on the same team. Period. The team is attempting to play against challenges in education, poverty, global competitiveness, public safety, etc. There's more than a full season of daunting challenges lined up and yet, when the team can't focus because of infighting, triumphs remain elusive.

This game-playing isn't lost on a dissatisfied electorate. The majority knows that political infighting results in lack of direction and efficacy, and that ignoring and excluding each other is a waste of intelligence and insight. Take California for example: Republican governor Arnold Schwarzenegger could not, or would not, work together with the Democratically-controlled legislature, and used that state's ballot-initiative process in an attempt to legislate directly with the electorate. What happened? Voters rejected his expensive end-run attempt around effective governance, and Schwarzenegger was dealt an embarrassing defeat on every initiative. He then hired a Democrat as his chief of staff, admittedly to the disappointment of those in his own party, who were clinging to him more for the party they shared than for his ability to govern effectively. He won reelection with a landslide victory.

Blind party allegiance is a waste of our capacity as complete and complex human beings. The electorate wants, and gets excited about, effective government; yet partisans in political leadership have been exhibiting traits that would get them kicked out of the leadership of any public company. Power struggling, undermining each other and hoarding authority are perceived as the weaknesses of middle management. This behavior is rarely exhibited, let alone tolerated, at the highest levels of successful corporations. In our political system as well, there is a growing weariness of divisive leadership, and polarizing leaders are seen as self-aggrandizing, petty, corrupt and dangerous. The electorate is tired of ineffectual leaders who are more focused on themselves and their party warfare than on outstanding governance.

Negotiating on the Same Side of the Table

We believe that political leadership is a series of negotiations on the same side of the table. To be clear, a team doesn't have to agree on everything. In fact, in a democracy, it's important that it doesn't. This form of government is based on the belief that it's crucial to pursue healthy debate so that minority opinions are heard and all representatives are able to make their highest contributions. When public collaboration is true teamwork, ideological opponents recognize that they are negotiating on the same side of the table. They then consistently place ego aside to constructively use the best of each other's ideas and inputs. This vision of collaboration makes party partisans archaic, their obstructive tactics abandoned in favor of thoughtful and productive opposition.

Very often, however, this scenario doesn't describe business as usual and, when communication has broken down into scandal, city leaders call on mediation and coaching to learn to work together. In our work with these groups, we provide a methodology for reframing the process toward collaboration and teamwork. We've found that successful political leaders make their contribution to graceful teamwork through a mastery of personal leadership—the ability to lead yourself. In our work with individual team members, we focus on five key aspects of personal leadership: self-knowledge and self-management, humility, courageous risk-taking, open-minded listening and mutual respect. We start with three modules focused on the clients' internal work – and follow up with two modules in which our clients are engaging others. All modules are key elements in developing emotional intelligence, evolving the capacity to lead this kind of change and craft your lasting contribution.

As we start talking about leadership, we want to expel any misconception that equates "strong leadership" with inflexibility and the characterization that equates open-mindedness and flexibility with "flip-flopping." Can you imagine where we would be today if all our scientists, explorers and researchers had to contend with being called a flip-flopper?

Our world would still be flat, the sun would revolve around the earth, and the moon would just be a circle of light in the sky untouched by human footprints. It is through the cultivated ability to advance our knowledge that we are able to better navigate our challenges, achieve our goals, and manifest our destiny. Truly strong

leaders are flexible, take a broad-minded approach, are decisive, and evolve not only their opinions but also their person. The key is communicating your strength to followers in a manner that inspires confidence rather than creating confusion and uncertainty.

Personal Leadership Mastery

Self-Knowledge and Self-Management
Sense of self is one of the most important traits of personal leadership. This awareness allows you to get to the best of yourself. By having a solid sense of self, any lingering insecurity can be translated into confidence. From this confidence, you can easily acknowledge that we are all human in our brilliance and vulnerability, and that none of us has all the answers.

A strong sense of self also gets to the core of your true values—your guiding principles. By knowing your values completely and beyond buzz words, you understand when your decisions are taking you away from your values and hampering your progress. Invite gifted people you respect to challenge your values and even yourself. Be willing to become confused and be suspicious if there aren't contrary opinions on your team, or even in your own mind, along the way. When you have a masterful grasp of your own values, you are infinitely better equipped to recognize when you may be justifying self-interest over the bigger vision and take the course corrections to stay true. When you take passion, conviction and purpose and marry them to compassion, you have Gandhi. When they are married to ego, you have Hitler.

Honest and unmerciful self-evaluation is an ongoing process that takes commitment. Delve deeply into exploring your strengths and weaknesses. For most people, seeing ourselves as weak can be scary. So once people create a list of 3-5 weaknesses, they often pat themselves on the back and take a breather at the very moment that it's crucial to keep going farther and digging more deeply. As Theodore Roosevelt said, "If you could kick the person in the pants responsible for most of your trouble, you wouldn't sit for a month." Examine what pushes your buttons, what causes you to lose perspective or spend time justifying to yourself. Watch your ego grapple for control when your pride is hurt. Know what triggers you to push others down rather than lifting them up. Go to the scary places and learn to genuinely feel fear and anger. Growing comfortable with yourself in the face of uncomfortable emotions permits you to respond thoughtfully, from a place of choice, and to communicate effectively in the face of fear or anger.

Genuine debates require not only the ability to express your viewpoint, but also to do so while processing your opponent's perspective and assimilating it into your own beliefs. Self-management in a heated discussion also allows you to fully engage others and show your best side. Especially since you want the same treatment.

You can also use curiosity to get past your own judgments in order to listen and perceive whether the other person feels just as deeply as you do. Use your compassion to understand how they are approaching the issue. Get beyond yourself to place a premium on teamwork and the integrity of the team as an entity. When you take this stance, you can shift any debate from a divisive bloodbath to a constructive engagement. Your teammates, even the ones who consider themselves your opponents, are disarmed, and you become known as the leader with a clear head who is committed to solutions and effective government. In other words, you can use this tool to become a true statesman.

Humility

> *Don't be humble ... you're not that great.*
> — Golda Meir

You don't need to know everything and have all the answers. You don't need to do everything right. In fact, it's important that you have screwed up and will do so again plenty of times. It means that you're out there taking risks instead of cowering and playing things too safe. Embrace your failures without judgment and unpack the most liberating and powerful tool in the toolbox: humility. This quality allows us to approach problems, situations and other people with an open and curious mind. We welcome new perspectives and new approaches to problems, but aren't led away from our vision because we're honest, we trust ourselves, and we stand rooted in our values. Instead of worrying about hiding our weaknesses, humility encourages us to augment them with the strengths of others. Sometimes a fresh and diametrically opposed perspective can give us important insights that we currently don't have.

We all know the times when we have left humility at the door, when we've been so certain of our solution and so eager to show our abilities and brilliance that humility was brushed aside by ego and pride. As a result, we didn't approach the situation with an open and curious mind, and did not fully understand or appreciate the problem. Because the solutions we were so committed to were not actually appropriate, we learned about humility by force rather than by choice.

When are you unable to be humble? Notice these times and learn from them. When does your ego get the better of you and prohibit you from admitting weaknesses or mistakes? To what lengths do you go to hide errors from others or, more importantly, from yourself? The saying, "What we can't live with runs our lives" means that, when push comes to shove, we will always make decisions based on what we're avoiding rather than what we want to embrace. To break out of this cycle in the area of humility, stop avoiding things about yourself that you don't want yourself or others to know. Start by stretching your humbleness with yourself. For example, take your biggest screw-up this week/month/year, and if you find judgment about yourself or others creeping in, use your curiosity to get to the learning. Ask yourself, "What can I learn from this mistake? What's the level of responsibility I can take for it that serves me best?"

When you've finished being curious, tell someone else about what happened. This isn't confession—you don't have to tell them all the gory details. This is just about sharing something with another person to get it out of your system. As Oscar Wilde said, "Life is too important to be taken seriously." Humility is powerful because it lets us be less critical toward ourselves, which in turn makes us a lot easier to work with and increases our mastery at teamwork.

Courageous Risk-Taking

Courageous risk-taking is what allows leaders to grow by pushing into new zones of discomfort and by developing resilience of character. This willingness and ability to stretch yourself is a key to achieving personal leadership and cultivating healthy confidence. You learn basketball by dribbling the ball with your dominant hand. Once that is achieved, you learn to dribble with your other hand. At first it seems awkward, but soon enough it becomes comfortable, and you're ready to dribble between the legs and around your back. Then you can really gain finesse.

But why should anyone take a risk in order to evolve and collaborate in the blood sport of politics? Quite frankly, that's what a leader does. Courage is found in the presence of purpose and the awareness of fear, not the absence of them. It takes courage to keep an open mind and engage ambiguity. The good thing is that courage breeds confidence in an upward cycle that can be infectious. The adrenaline, learning and personal growth you experience to achieve a courageous breakthrough have addictive qualities. Our greatest leaders didn't become legends by playing things safe; they took risk after persistent risk, they did not conform to standards and, at some point, they got the big win.

How often are you pushing your limits? Find a way to do that every day and every week. Eleanor Roosevelt's voice encourages us to "do one thing every day that frightens you." These things can be small or large, and each will continue to develop your personal leadership abilities. What can you teach your team about being courageous and taking risks? How can this be your leadership contribution?

Open-Minded Listening

The founding fathers of the American Republic used a Native American tradition taught to them by chiefs of the Iroquois Federation to create empathetic listening. At the heart of it is the Talking Stick.

A Talking Stick gives the holder of the stick the right to talk without interruption until they feel that their listeners clearly understand their point. The listeners may not argue, agree or disagree; all they can do is articulate that they understand by restating the speaker's point in a way that the speaker becomes confident that there is real understanding, not just patronizing acknowledgment. Then the speaker passes the Talking Stick to the next person to make their points. Imagine how different your day might be if you were packing a Talking Stick!

Since being heard is a fundamental need that regularly goes unmet, listening without an agenda is a great tool for building relationships. It allows you to gain new insights, create allies and build the respect of peers who may have little in common with you. Listening to another, empathizing and putting yourself in their proverbial shoes is ancient wisdom that enables you to cultivate the willingness in others to collaborate with you. This in turn allows you to champion a process dedicated to bringing together multiple perspectives in service of a great collaborative solution. When you don't listen, you deny yourself the opportunity to evolve and achieve that new understanding that could break through an impasse.

To get a fresh understanding of your colleagues, your staff or your spouse, start by recognizing the assumptions you use in filtering what is being said in any conversation. Put them aside, and listen as if you've just met in order to hear what's actually being said, instead of what you expect to hear.

Mutual Respect

When we let go of assumptions, a disagreement in one area will not be the sole basis of your opinion of another's capability. Demonstrating respect this way creates the desire to find common ground, which is the foundation for collaboration.

You can build mutual respect by observing the times you judge others' motivations, abilities and limitations. Are you using some sort of shorthand, like how they are dressed, where they went to school or what beliefs they hold? Recognize yourself doing this, and know that, even if you consider yourself a great judge of people, you are coming to the wrong conclusion more frequently than you realize.

When you take a stand for mutual respect, you can more easily create allies to achieve team-based solutions. Collaboration is open mindedness meeting broad-based input to create intensive, durable commitments for mutual gain. To become a better collaborator, seek commonalities, and acknowledge and explore differences, instead of being immobilized by them. Seeking commonalities starts with agreeing on common goals. Any tendency to focus on infighting and the differences we hold is ineffectual, petty and, well, human – albeit not one of our more positive traits.

It is easy for us to create allies who share our dislikes and opinions. It automatically becomes more difficult when we perceive someone as different because of our own judgments or stereotyping. However, these differences often hold the spark for innovative solutions. Create alliances that allow you to brainstorm candidly and honestly about solutions without having to trade horses or be concerned with threats of media leaks. Environments like this are the foundation for our most capable minds to solve our most daunting problems.

Get a Reputation

When political leaders make the effort to really work these principles, they get a reputation. Respect grows among their colleagues, which turns into genuine collaboration. Engaged citizens are drawn to a politician who meets their hopes for leadership and exceeds their expectations. When a broken team soaked in scandal really works these principles, we coaches happily find ourselves out of a job.

And if you are wondering what you alone can do to turn things around, remember: One person with a vision can be an incredibly powerful force. Cultivate allies who share your vision and your impact becomes stronger. Enough momentum to create a tipping point is created when as little as 3% of the people are on board. It takes only one individual with vision, courage and determination to bring that 3% together.

Be that *one*.

Apply the Insight – Build Your Team

Who would you be uncomfortable approaching to engage in a simple, neutral, collegial conversation? Take our challenge and invite that person to lunch! Foster mutual respect by discharging your stereotypes, listening with fresh ears and looking for areas of alignment. Then keep doing this again and again until you can easily engage with anyone on either side of the aisle.

The Gumption Partners
Michelle Randall, MBA, PCC
Chad White, MBA
408.782.1703
michelle@glasshousescoaching.com
chad@brauercapital.com

The Gumption Partners is a collaboration between Michelle Randall and Chad White that specializes in interventions repairing communication among city council members through an emphasis on personal leadership.

Michelle Randall is CEO of Glass Houses Coaching & Consulting, Inc., which serves people in the public eye, specifically political leaders, and their families and staff. She is an engaged citizen and a nonpartisan coach. In other words, she coaches her clients, not their politics. Michelle holds a BA from Eleanor Roosevelt College at the University of California San Diego, and a Masters of Business Administration from the Monterey Institute of International Studies. She is a Professional Certified Coach and a member of the International Coach Federation. She is coauthor of *Visionary Women Inspiring the World: 12 Paths to Personal Power* (Skyward).

Chad White is a consultant in turnaround management. He is the managing partner of a private equity firm that invests in underperforming companies. Chad holds a BSE in biomedical engineering from Duke University and a Masters of Business Administration from Vanderbilt University, and he has completed the requirements for a Masters of Science in Taxation at Georgia State University. In addition, he is a member of the MLF Client Office, which consults and assists wealthy families with the challenges and opportunities of wealth transfer between generations through leadership and stewardship.

This partnership exhibits true bipartisanship between a dyed-in-the-wool Democrat and a committed Republican who regularly engage in passionate policy discussions. The gloves are off, but there is always an underlying mutual respect and commitment to solving issues that make a difference to their families, businesses, community and world.

Getting Unstuck

Heather Cummings Jensen

A democracy is like a relationship, is like a shark, as Woody
Allen says. A shark dies unless it is moving. A relationship dies
unless it's moving—that's the Woody Allen part. Democracy is
like that. It dies unless it is coevolving with power.
Because power is always evolving.
— Robert W. Fuller, *Somebodies and Nobodies*

Our political systems today need leaders who can help democracy continue to evolve. Leaders who understand the importance of movement to the vitality of a country. Leaders who can lead us through the places where our countries get stuck. In other words, leaders who can be like sharks.

As a visionary political leader, you certainly sense the public hunger for the evolution of politics and our democratic systems. This hunger for something different is well documented in Richard C. Harwood's *Hope Unraveled.* Harwood tracks the trend of unraveling hope from 1990 to 2003 through conversations he's had in communities in the United States. His research shows the following pattern:

- In 1990, the public felt pushed out of politics by special-interest groups, sensational news media and the sense that politicians were just out to serve their own interests.
- In 1992, the public was still angry about politics, but now worried that the system itself could not address the growing challenges of their concerns.
- In 1995, the public's anger gave way to deep lament because they felt their concerns were not being addressed.
- By 1998, people had decided to retreat from politics and public life. They found comfort in closely-knit circles of families and friends. This narrower focus helped them regain a sense of control over their changing lives.
- In 2003, people felt deeply frustrated by the false start toward repairing the nation's politics and public life after September 11, 2001.

When you look at this feedback from these communities across the United States, it's easy to conclude, at least from one perspective, that our practice of politics and democracy is stuck. If democracy is like a shark and needs to stay moving to stay alive, what could this mean for you as a leader?

Before we explore this question further, let's take a look at why sharks need to keep moving. Researchers have found that sharks die if they aren't in motion, because they absorb oxygen into their gills and breathe through their forward movement. Research has also discovered that if salmon sharks stop swimming, their muscles will stiffen, making them dormant and in danger of never regaining movement. Since they keep themselves warm by moving, they die if they stop.

You may be reading this and thinking to yourself, "Hey, I've got this shark thing down. I'll never die; I have the nonstop schedule of someone in politics!" While this is true, you need to remember that the principle of balance is also inherent in the life of a shark. You can experience this by doing a little experiment.

Put this book down for a moment and stand up. Balance yourself on one foot. Notice that, to stay balanced on that foot, you must constantly move. If, as you balance on your foot, one area gets a little heavy, you make a small adjustment to bring yourself back to balance. While the moves may be slight, you are still constantly moving for balance.

This same principle of balance works in our lives: If you're worn out and exhausted from your work, you can spend a bit of time resting or doing something fun and, sure enough, your energy and vitality returns to your work life. If you make a choice to focus your attention elsewhere, energy returns to the area of your life that needed a break.

This is where being a like a shark can help your political leadership. When we're stuck on something in our lives, we tend to see only one possibility, a single position. We often forget about moving around, exploring other options, seeing other perspectives.

It's in these moments when we are stuck that our countries need shark-like leaders—leaders who are attuned to the aliveness of the political system and know how to move in ways that explore and nurture possibilities. This kind of leadership is less about what you do and more about who you are willing to be. Are you willing to explore and invite others to experiment with possibilities? Are you willing to invite yourself and others to access your ability to choose not just from the one option most obvious, but from all other possibilities?

Have you ever had the experience in a group where you made a statement that no one else had mentioned? You may even have felt shy or hesitant to say it, but you did it nonetheless. Then, as soon as the words were out of your mouth, people jumped into the conversation, saying that they had been thinking the same thing but were afraid to say something or were unsure of what they were feeling but you named it for them? People will often be relieved that someone told the hard truth and is willing to provide the leadership to take them to a new place.

There are many signals that a project or perspective on an issue could use an infusion of new energy:

- No action is being taken.
- People say, "It's the way things are."
- There's a feeling of being overwhelmed.
- "The way things are" is all other people's fault.
- The same situation keeps happening over and over again.
- People are giving up.

The act of noticing and naming the narrowness of a viewpoint is radical, both because of the courage it can take to specify the hard truth, and because, in naming an attitude, you are asserting that there are other perspectives from which to choose.

It is your ability to recognize choices that makes you a potent leader. When you step outside the limits of how you thought you should do something, you will not only have a positive impact on your own life, but you will also have a ripple effect on others. When you help others access their ability to choose from outside their narrow points of view, you help them connect with their powerfulness and their ability to see the world beyond the narrow options they thought they had.

So how do you bring this aliveness and awareness of choice to your life as a political leader? Let's do a little coaching here. Normally, we would be doing this by phone rather than through the written word, and I would ask questions that are just for you, building on what you have said before or where the energy and aliveness comes from your reflections. Also, if we were coaching one-on-one, you would bring to our call the topic that we're coaching on today, and I would not be setting the agenda of our conversation.

In the absence of being together on the phone, I'll take you through a process that will help you bring a new perspective to an issue or a problem. If the direction I'm going interests you, read on. If it doesn't have juice for you, skip this chapter for now. It will be here if your interest peaks later.

If you're still with me, let's get started.

STEP ONE: Recognize that you are stuck.

This is probably the hardest step of all, because we can think so thoroughly that "there are no other alternatives" that we don't realize we are stuck in an attitude.

Use these statements as a kickoff for pinpointing a situation in which you may be stuck:

- There's only one way to get ahead in this party.
- The right and/or left are so entrenched in their views that they'll never come around on this issue.
- Citizens just don't understand.
- To win, you have to raise lots of money.

Other places to look:

- Where do you feel overwhelmed?
- What are you avoiding thinking about?
- Where are you disappointed or frustrated?

As you consider where you are stuck, you may become tired. Your spirit may go from uplifted to downtrodden. Even as I'm writing this, I am not sure that I want to keep typing. This is the heavy, static energy of being stuck. I'm pointing this out to help you identify places where you are stuck in the future. Because we can take the status quo for granted and not challenge it, it's helpful to know the feeling of being stuck so we can recognize it emotionally if not cognitively.

So do you have in mind a situation where you are stuck? If nothing is coming to you, choose something that you want to brainstorm.

Before we go further, I want to validate the utter humanness of being stuck. It's something that all of us, from all walks of life, have experienced at some time to varying degrees. There's absolutely nothing wrong with feeling stuck.

So, with your situation in mind, experience the range of emotions you feel around this situation. They could include hopelessness, resignation, fear, frustration, anger, disappointment or a variety of other feelings. Give yourself a minute to really *feel*. There's no judgment here; whatever is true for you, let yourself feel it.

You might notice now that things have shifted a bit. You may feel another level of emotion, or you may feel relieved that you have had a chance to just be with what you've been feeling.

Next, notice any assumptions you may have. For instance, you may assume that you will have to work around the situation where you are stuck, or that nothing can happen because of what feels like a certain reality. What assumptions do you have about your situation?

Give yourself some time to reflect. What's important now is to begin to acknowledge that this angle is just one possible slant from which to view the situation.

While this is an article about getting unstuck, there is no judgment if you decide that you want to stay stuck. After all, the core of this article is about exploring options so that you can choose. Staying stuck can actually be useful at times, especially when we take the time to look around and explore "stuckness" and ask:

- What do I want to happen that is not?
- What can I learn from being here?

So, before you move further on this coaching exercise, I want you to make a conscious decision about whether you want to remain stuck or shake up your thinking a bit. If now is the right time to explore your options for this situation, stay with me. Otherwise, I encourage you to milk your stuckness for all it's worth!

STEP TWO: Name the perspective you are in.

Since you've decided you're willing to play with some options, take a minute to name both the situation where you are stuck and the particular perspective you have on it.

For instance, if I said, "The right and/or left are so entrenched in their views that they'll never come around on this issue," the situation in which I am stuck is "moving forward on an issue." The perspective I have around the situation might be called "hopeless."

STEP THREE: Explore other perspectives.

Now that you are clear about where you are, it's time to be a shark. You're moving out of "this is the one and only way of seeing things" into other possibilities. By moving around and trying different hats, you'll create energy and aliveness.

Begin to brainstorm other viewpoints around your situation besides the perspective you currently have.

For instance, in my example of getting agreement on an issue where there are entrenched views, some possible alternatives to my "hopeless" perspective could be the viewpoint of:

- A curious bystander
- Someone turned off by politics
- Someone with an entrenched point of view
- A child

In this case, I have used different types of people, but don't restrict yourself. You could be playful and explore how different kinds of cars might respond to your situation. A fast sports car would bring different qualities than a convertible or an S.U.V. Often, the more playful you are, the more freedom and possibility you open up!

Now that you have these different perspectives, you can try them out and see how they might apply to your situation. For example:

A **curious bystander** might move forward by asking a lot of questions, stepping back and observing, feeling unattached to the outcome, and reserving all judgment.

Someone turned off by politics might move forward by wanting to know how the issue matters to their friends and family. While they don't have faith in the political process, they wouldn't want leaders to offer any false hope.

Someone with an entrenched point of view might move forward but care only about the people they feel accountable to, wanting to know that you and the rest of the world share their passion, or at least will resolve the issue from their perspective.

A child might move forward by keeping things in simple language, caring about other people's feelings, and being totally willing to tell the truth with childlike innocence.

When you explore your perspectives, what do you find?

Notice that, when you are taking on a viewpoint, you are not trying to fix or solve the problem that is causing the stuckness. Instead, you are looking at different views of how you could interact with the situation.

STEP FOUR: Decide the way you want to move forward

You've explored different ways you could approach your situation. In this step, you choose the attitude you want to take.

There may be one perspective that stands out as the way forward, or you may want to combine aspects of the perspectives you like and make up an entirely new one.

In my example, rather than "hopeless," I might choose a view that includes:

- Stepping back and observing
- Being curious about the passion around the issue
- Caring about the feelings of others
- Telling the truth

Choosing who you want to be as a leader creates the energy and movement of the shark. You are not accepting the uncontested conventional wisdom or even your own usual ways of being. By doing this, you are keeping relationships, and ultimately democracy, alive and vital. You are adding new oxygen as you swim forward, and keeping your muscles warm and flexible so you can be responsive to what's needed.

This kind of leadership is exciting; it energizes politics. This kind of leadership can transform a country from resignation to hope.

Can you feel the shift in the nature of my writing as you read? You may be smiling. You may feel hopeful. You may be energized yourself. Notice what feeling has been evoked in you as you read these last few paragraphs. This is the kind of impact you will have on people when you consciously choose the perspective from which you want to lead. You are that powerful and you make that much of a difference.

STEP FIVE: Make it real.

Once you've decided the perspective you want to take moving forward, it's time to make a plan and get into action.

The plan doesn't have to be extensive. But it's helpful to know what you are saying Yes to doing and what you are saying No to doing when you act from this new perspective. Make a quick list:

What I am saying Yes to:	What I am saying No to:
1.	
2.	
3.	
4.	

Can you feel the energy of this declaration? Now, what will your next steps be, and by when will you have them done?

I challenge you to set this book down and take that first action.

Coevolving with Your Own Power

Many have said that, in the wake of the Civil Rights movement, our culture has moved to one of entitlement, and we are focused on our rights with little care about our responsibility as citizens.

The irony is that, whether we are citizens or leaders, we often take only a narrow view of what's possible, yet when we take responsibility for our perspectives and choices, we gain greater freedom.

Robert Fuller, cited earlier, admonishes us that democracy must coevolve with power. I urge you, as a political leader, to coevolve with your own power. Essential to this is knowing that you are fully responsible for how you show up in the world and that you have a choice in what that looks like. In refusing to be stuck in stereotypes of political leaders or the lowered expectations of the public, you energize our political system and contribute to its ongoing evolution.

Make a list of where you are stuck in your political life. Take one issue and run through the process outlined above.

The author gratefully acknowledges the contribution of The Coaches Training Institute and their Balance Model to her insight on exploring a variety of perspectives.

Self-Mastery and Political Power

Sam House and Anne Fifield

We've observed that the source of personal power is not where most people believe it to be. To wield influence requires more than official authority, and true greatness lies beyond the glossy presentation political figures enjoy in the media today. True greatness requires a deep connection to your personal power while using it in service of others.

We also believe that great leaders are not born, but made. And that is good news, considering the current state we citizens find ourselves in. Our current political climate maligns flexibility as "flip-flopping" and favors competition over collaboration. In this era of bipartisan spin, there is a wholesale crisis of confidence in our political leaders.

We assume you're concerned about finding a strategy that works to promote your ideas (i.e. "winning"), and yet we suspect you are wondering whether you can play the game differently. We believe you're interested in a higher level of sportsmanship than what you see on the playing field around you, and that you want to address the current leadership crisis and be part of a different, better generation of leaders.

If these assumptions are correct, read on. In this chapter, we offer you a new way to consider power, a deep appreciation for the role of emotional intelligence in leadership, and a handle on specific tools you can begin using as soon as you finish reading.

A Crisis of Confidence in Our Leadership

This has been one of the most disappointing eras of leadership in our history.

Across the political spectrum, from locally elected officials to the nation's president or prime minister, our well of trust in our political leaders has run dry. And why not? The scandals, lies and corruption of the last decade have given us plenty of reasons to be cynical. From the dishonesty of Bill Clinton in the Monica Lewinsky scandal to the pretenses the Bush administration has given for invading Iraq, our political leaders have attempted to twist things to their own advantage while disregarding the impact of telling such lies on the collective consciousness of our nation.

As a result, we no longer trust our leaders to protect or inform us. And this loss of trust causes us to become angry and unwilling to work together, or we tune out entirely, focus on our busy lives, and become apathetic to the important issues facing us. The notion of political integrity in this climate has become either a joke or, more disturbingly, a fond memory. Often it seems it no longer matters if what a political leader says, and what he or she does, are consistent.

Politicians today script responses to every conceivable situation that might arise, believing that with enough foresight and planning, they will be able to "manage" the situation, do damage control, or curry favor. The heavy influence of "spin" is all-important. To mention politicians and integrity in the same sentence elicits skepticism, even laughter. But this issue is by no means a laughing matter or something that can simply be disregarded. At no point in history has it been clearer that we *must* move toward authenticity at all levels of the political spectrum—from first-tier staffers to elected officials.

There is a nationwide hunger for our leaders to demonstrate authenticity. This yearning for frankness by the public is finding new ways of demanding honest expression by political leaders. The mushrooming number of political blogs is proof that citizens are continuing to search for a source they can trust for the truth, or at least a place where the hard questions are asked and explored.

This ongoing drive to create a deeper awareness of the political landscape can't be stifled or "managed" through spin control. A recent *New York Times* headline heralded the arrival of "The YouTube Election." YouTube is an internet video site where ordinary citizens post contributions, either journalistic or entertaining (or both). Several political candidates have already been embarrassed by being caught on tape making statements contrary to the ones they publicly profess. "Candidates, Be Careful: Someone Is Taping" warned the caption over the responses on the op-ed page to the article. In her letter to the *Times* editor, citizen Helen Pfeffer writes, "I look forward to the day when candidates are pushed so far into their 'scripted bubble' that some of them bust right out the other side, revealing themselves to be smart, decent, hard-working people who would rather represent their constituents than play a politician on TV."

Regardless of whether it comes from blogs or mainstream news sources, the public's persistent hunger for truth, honesty and authenticity from our political leaders is real and enduring. The question is: how will our leaders respond?

The response of our leaders to the public's crisis of faith in the political process has produced behavior that is creating a vicious circle. To appease the public's concern about their capability, leaders have redoubled their efforts to look unassailable. This has led to increased testing of political messages, more secrecy and protectiveness on the part of candidates, and less flexibility and spontaneity when speaking extemporaneously. But people are not roped in by the spin; in fact, they can see right through it. There is a better way. It is called, quite simply, telling the truth.

Honesty is STILL the Best Policy

> *Character is the only secure foundation of the state.*
> — Calvin Coolidge, 30th American President

Our on-the-spot, 24-hours-a-day news culture has raised the bar for the need to be honest and authentic at all times. TV cameras and microphones capture political leaders' every word and broadcast them to the world just moments later. In this environment, being honest is not just a morally sound practice; it's a competitive advantage. It's also simpler and less expensive than the alternative. From a practical point of view, lies or "incomplete truths" are exhausting to maintain and protect. If you've hidden something, you need to *continue* hiding it, for as long as you need it to remain out of view. The act of hiding may itself require hiding, and that requires yet more effort.

But "not lying," or refraining from moral error, is a narrow definition of honesty. And for the well-intentioned, outright lies are not the problem. More of you will struggle with the larger grey area of accidental lies, incomplete truths, and mistakes. As a political leader, you work with incomplete information *at all times*. Because of the complexity of the decisions you make, you rely on others to inform you. And one of your great potential liabilities is receiving incorrect or incomplete information. So mistakes—and the subsequent need to take a new position—are inherent in the work you do. The question is: how will you handle the inevitable mistakes that occur?

Answer for them—quickly and publicly. When you recover, and "course correct" openly, you show others that you are accountable, vigilant about your integrity, and keeping track of what you'd promised. Admitting responsibility and apologizing publicly shows others that they can trust you. When you publicly admit fault and are open about wanting to improve, you send the message to your constituents that you are working *together*. Also, when you model honesty, you encourage it in the people around you. And as a politician, you NEED to train the people you work with to be as honest as possible, because you rely on them for critical information. Being honest, even when—*especially* when—the news is difficult to deliver, or unwanted, or when there has been a failure, is critical to keeping others' trust in you.

Doing otherwise is tempting, but dangerous. As we now know, when we, as a public, feel lied to, we become angry and mistrustful or apathetic. In either case, we become splintered. We no longer have the will to work together. For any kind of political leader, this spells disaster, because political leadership is the art of engaging and uniting people. And this requires both courage and emotional intelligence.

Case in Point

During the Bay of Pigs invasion, things did not go as planned. President Kennedy decided to stand in front of the nation and take the heat. Faulty planning by the previous administration's CIA director resulted in a disastrous invasion and 1500 deaths. President Kennedy stood up publicly, took full responsibility, and apologized to the nation. And then an unexpected thing happened: his popularity soared. National trust in the President soared as a direct result of his courage to admit error. Lives were lost but the public's trust was preserved.

Authenticity and the Paradox of Power

> *To be natural is such a very difficult pose to keep up.*
> — Oscar Wilde

Being forthright, or forthcoming, is an active form of truth-telling. This is what people mean when they speak of transparency—an active revealing of what's within. When we can see how something works, we feel we know its nature.

Does revealing your mistakes and openly expressing your emotional reactions to your environment sound daunting? It does to most people. When you tell the truth, there's nowhere to hide, no other position to retreat to. This can feel vulnerable, and people often hold back because they don't like feeling so exposed. You may wonder, "How on earth can that kind of vulnerability possibly be powerful?"

This apparent contradiction is the paradox of power. It seems counter-intuitive to be vulnerable or revealing just when you want to summon every shred of strategic protection. We can see this paradox at work in the physical world: when we are young, we are taught to "fall softly" to avoid getting hurt. The urge to protect ourselves causes us to tense. Similarly, "tensing" emotionally can make us less flexible, and less able to respond. Relaxation on the other hand, gives us full range of motion, and faster access to a full range of responses. Steering into a skid on a snowy winter road is another example of a counter-intuitive, but effective, moment to surrender. The martial art of aikido is based on a similar concept. Opponents will not block your punch; if they can, they will grab it and pull you, using the direction of your force to their advantage.

In leadership, there is power in expressing vulnerability, but this power is rarely employed for fear of appearing "weak." As a culture, we associate vulnerability with shame and call it "weakness." And yet, think of those rare times when a public figure has risked being vulnerable without accompanying it with self-smearing shame. A person admitting their faults or omissions with head held high, offering whatever truth needs to be told, is a powerful image. Why?

Authenticity is inspiring because it allows people to see themselves in you, and feel personally connected to you. As a political leader (and you *are* a leader, whether you are a staffer, a chief of staff or an elected official), you can present a focus-grouped version of yourself. Or you can tell the truth and be authentic—consistently. Not just the facts related to the world of your actions, but also the truth of your strongest convictions and your highest values. Bring your richly developed authentic self to the table and watch the ease with which you influence others. On the contrary, bring that faux cutout of yourself—the one that looks like everyone else around you—and watch how ineffective you are at influencing others to share your view. It's your choice.

Continually bringing your *real* self forward is what creates a compelling leader. What's your *unique* way of bringing inspiration to the game you're playing? People often get their notion of what it means to be inspiring from watching others. Yet the qualities that endear you to others—or inspire them—may be your peculiar ways of doing things, or your unusual perspective. In any case, they are unique to you. And yet you may have spent your life trying to fit yourself into a mold built for others (apparent cool competence, for example). It's time to gain some appreciation for your true style of operating in the world—and do more of that. When you become congruent with who you are, you develop the ability to authentically inspire others, and win not only their minds, but also their hearts.

Case in Point

Al Gore exhibited the power of authenticity immediately after his run for the presidency in 2000. Throughout the election, he was seen as dry, wooden, impersonal, and overly intellectual. He tried to appear calm, clear and "presidential" as he attempted to create a public image that he thought would be favored by voters. All too often, he stuck to safe comments that would not cause much controversy. It was not until his concession speech at the end of the election that the public got to see an Al Gore unfettered by concern for public opinion. Free to be passionate, fiery and heartfelt, Gore made one of his finest speeches. The pundits were amazed. The voters exclaimed, "Where was *that* man during the campaign? I would have voted for him!" No longer worried about looking good, Gore spoke from his heart, fully expressing his values instead of pulling his punches. Though not a candidate for the '08 presidential race at this writing, he is seen by many voters as a top candidate because he continues to be clearly connected to his values—and speaks passionately and authentically, without attempting to be approved of by anyone.

Leaders Are Not Born, But Made

> *The virtues of men are of more consequence to society than their abilities; and for this reason, the heart should be cultivated with more [diligence] than the head.*
> — Noah Webster, *On the Education of Youth in America*, 1788

Effective leadership requires a strong emotional intelligence (EQ). While IQ, or raw intellectual intelligence, is important for political leaders, countless studies have shown that it is the leader with a strong EQ who is most likely to achieve powerful results consistently and enjoy long-lasting influence. Intellectual characteristics that have been celebrated historically, and which have been thought to represent the pinnacle of greatness in leaders, are now understood to be no more important—and maybe less so—than a leader's ability to connect compassionately and authentically with others. This ability, expressed in beautiful and rare moments in public arenas, is what wins people's loyalty and trust. The moment of stepping courageously out to express one's self authentically is the moment when true leadership begins.

The Key to Emotional Intelligence: Listening

> *The secret of success is to do*
> *the common things uncommonly well.*
> — John D. Rockefeller

Listening—and the awareness it demands—is arguably the foundation of emotional intelligence. Self-awareness, self-management, initiative, innovation, adaptability, empathy, collaboration, and other leadership skills, come from careful listening. The ability to listen deeply and be aware of emotions—the ones that lie within you, as well as the ones that permeate the relationships you are involved in—is also a hallmark of great leadership.

The political arena is filled with people who have ideas and who fight for those ideas to be accepted. There is a sense of urgency: "If I don't push hard enough or speak loudly enough, I won't be heard." The arena then fills with a cacophony of voices. With everyone screaming to have their ideas heard, there is no one to listen to them.

There is a difference between listening and merely hearing: listening is active. In masterful listening, you consciously control where you put your attention. Great leaders listen, both to the spoken voices and to the unspoken energy of the surrounding environment. With this awareness, they can answer both the information being conveyed and to what is in the "emotional field." This ability to identify and speak to what's going on has an immediate and powerful impact on the field itself.

Case in Point

Often, when there is anger in the emotional field and the leader is aware of it, the very act of naming it helps to dissipate it. When Robert Kennedy learned of the death of Martin Luther King Jr., he was on a flight to Indianapolis during the 1968 Presidential campaign. Immediately after landing at the airport he addressed an angry crowd of mostly African-Americans. Aware of their feelings, Kennedy spoke directly to the near-riotous anger and outrage that was present in the energy of the emotional field. By doing so—instead of sticking to the safer content of a prepared script—he was able to be both vulnerable and powerful, and directly acknowledge the public's range of intense emotions with a profound sense of empathy.

For the sake of training you to listen powerfully as a leader, we will introduce you to a model that offers distinctions between different kinds of listening. In this model, there are three levels of listening: internal, focused on other, and global. Each level demands a different kind of awareness, and each level will help you develop different aspects of emotional intelligence, and create different kinds of alignment.

Listening at Level 1: Internal

Courage is what it takes to stand up and speak; courage is also what it takes to sit down and listen.
—Winston Churchill

At Level 1 the focus is on you. When you listen at Level 1, you hear the words of others, but you're really listening to your own inner thoughts, ideas and opinions. You assess what others are saying with an eye toward the impact or insight their words will have for you. This internal focus can create invaluable awareness, but it is not enough on its own to create leadership, let alone dialogue.

It is enough to foster a number of aspects of emotional intelligence, however. Self-awareness is born from Level 1 listening, and well-applied, this can lead to a more accurate self-assessment and better self-management. When you listen at Level 1 you know your own mind; you are aware of your values, your preferences, your fears, and your stake in a conversation. Knowing yourself is a prerequisite to having others know you, and so it is also the basis of honest connection and transparency.

Level 1 is where your can access your intuition, your moral compass, and your commitment. As you speak and act, this is where you will sense your internal congruence. It's also where you'll sense self-betrayal. When you're pushing too hard, speaking without adequate conviction or knowledge, trying to look good, or in any way hiding or compromising yourself, you'll sense it here. And when you self-correct, your internal compass—accessed through Level 1 listening—is what you'll steer by.

While Level 1 introspection is valuable, it's a terrible place to spend your time in a conversation if you want to learn about someone else. When you talk with someone, and you are at Level 1, you're not really in a conversation, despite the exchange of words. You're really just delivering an interrupted monologue. While you're listening to you, you're certainly not listening to them; you're thinking only of what you want to say next, your opinion of their ideas, the way you are dressed, or your next meeting, etc. This is, unfortunately, the level at which most "listening" occurs in our culture. This is also the level at which most political debate and discourse occurs.

In the United States, there is a growing swell of discontent with news shows that emphasize the drama created between two "talking heads" with opposing political views, barking out their own agendas while showing no interest or awareness of the agenda of the other. The act of one political leader interacting with another while only listening at Level 1 is remarkably similar to watching two children playing in a sandbox, chatting in parallel monologues, with no real interaction and exchange.

The public is eager for you, as a political leader, to move beyond the spectacle of listening at Level I only. We want to see you advocate for your own ideas AND acknowledge and engage the ideas of those who disagree with you. We want dialogue.

Apply the Insight: Level I
Notice where you are in conversation.

- Pick a difficult situation you are facing, and ask yourself, "What do I want?" Drop into Level 1 listening and notice what thoughts arise in answer to this question. Now drop deeper into yourself. Be aware of your body. What effect do these thoughts have on you? Notice your feelings.
- Catch yourself today caught up in your own thoughts when other people are speaking. When you notice this, practice recovering openly, and say something like, "I'm sorry, I was thinking of something else for a moment and I want to understand what you said. Would you say that again?"

Listening at Level 2: Other

When you are listening at Level 2, you shift away from your own thoughts to concentrate fully on the words and ideas of the person in front of you. You're fueled by curiosity, motivated to discover the meaning of the conversation for the person you're listening to. Focused so completely on the other person's perspective, you become unconcerned about your own need to be heard, and you lose awareness of your own thoughts, concerns, judgments, etc.

Level 2 listening is the birthplace of empathy, a critical component of emotional intelligence. When you do not redirect the conversation to yourself, and instead focus your observations and commentary to what you notice about the other, that person has a chance to feel seen and heard. When they start to feel known by you, a bridge begins to form between you. This is the basis of trust—a prerequisite to having your peers and constituents follow your lead.

When you are focused on people in this way, you can make them feel acknowledged and empowered. Giving powerful, heartfelt acknowledgments is an essential skill for an emotionally intelligent leader. An acknowledgment goes deeper than a compliment. A compliment praises a *result*; an acknowledgement recognizes the quality within someone that *generated* the result. As a leader, it's your privilege to want people to shine in the world and in the work they do. Engage with their greatness. Be willing to share the stage, so the hidden talents of others can be brought forth and used in unforeseen ways.

Apply the Insight: Level 2
Use Focused Listening.

* Practice articulating out loud what you are hearing the other person say. Notice their reactions. How accurately did you interpret their words?

* Practice giving powerful acknowledgments. Pick someone you want to connect to, or who needs to hear from you. Go inside yourself for a moment (Level 1) and connect with some aspect of the person that truly moves you. It doesn't have to be profound; it may be something very small, but nonetheless inspiring to you. Now stand in front of the person and tell them—from the very center of your heart and with no apology—what moves you about them. Stay focused on them (Level 2) and notice the impact.

Listening at Level 3: Global

When you listen at Level 3, your focus is on the space around you. Your attention is on the other, but with a softer focus. You are also aware of the environment: the temperature in the room, the sounds in the background—and most importantly—the energy of the emotions present in the room that can be felt between you and the person, or people, you're speaking to.

Level 3 listening may sound a bit conceptual, but it's actually basic, and intuitive. Most people have an awareness of Level 3 already; they just don't access it consciously. It's somewhere between what directors and actors call "subtext," and something more visceral—an intuition informed by animal instinct. Level 3 awareness is that sensibility that allows us to tell the difference between an awkward silence, and a thoughtful one. Your Level 3 awareness is on when you suddenly notice it's not only quiet, but the energy in the room is completely still and "you could hear a pin drop."

When you're listening at Level 3, you're aware of how this energy changes constantly, which enhances your ability to recover when you are off-base or have said something that was misunderstood or created disagreement.

Apply the Insight: Level 3
Notice what's "in the air."

- As you listen to people today, look beyond their words to their emotional state. How do they feel about what they're saying? What are they *not* saying? Be curious. What else is going on in the room besides the obvious interaction? Are people restless or attentive? Begin to consciously check your sense of the space around you and see what information it contains.

Powerful leaders listen at Level 3 and respond authentically to what they hear or sense in the environment. Those who are good at conveying their awareness are instantly appreciated for this ability to tune in to others, read the energy, and respond effectively. The capacity to lead a group comes from this level of awareness and listening.

Level 3 listening fosters the emotional intelligence skills of collaboration, conflict resolution and creating alignment. When you're listening at Level 3, you can more easily see how to bring people together. And if you're leading in a group, organization, community, or polity, you will *always* need to bring people together. By keeping your awareness on the energy in the room, you can help parties align around a common stake and move toward resolution.

You are unafraid to bring conflict to light because you know that conflict is a natural and normal part of ANY human process. In fact, it is needed at times to clarify positions and help people remember what they care deeply about. The presence of conflict is an opportunity to bring to the surface well-intentioned passions that have become waylaid by their less-than-ideal expression. When these passions have risen to the surface, you work adeptly at honoring ALL of the voices speaking, and you model and create respect, understanding, and when possible, alignment. Once people can see where they are aligned, the need for complete agreement becomes less necessary.

Apply the Insight
Practice the power of "and."

- Reflect the intention to collaborate in your speech by observing what is valuable or interesting about what people say to you, and only then adding any commentary or concerns you have. Use the word "and" instead of "but" before you add your own ideas. "And" is inclusive, whereas "but" subjects everything before it to the concern that follows it, giving the second half of the sentence greater weight. *Tip*: Stay at Level 2, curious about what the other person is saying, until you find something to genuinely appreciate. If they seem defensive, or negative, look more deeply: what value do they think they are protecting?

As Stephen Covey says "first seek to understand, then to be understood." When we are looking at a thorny issue, we must acknowledge that many points of view have validity. We may heartily disagree over which choice is better, but if I embrace the notion that I am right and you are wrong we only continue to polarize the conversation. When we become aware that each perspective on an issue has something to offer, and is therefore "legitimate," we can begin to align ourselves on common ground.

Imagine presenting your cogent argument in the next political debate, AND showcasing your ability to truly listen to your opponent and respond with a forthright, clear and observable awareness of their position (i.e., you demonstrate awareness and listening at Levels 2 and 3), rather than simply forcing a single-minded agenda (Level 1) with no visible interaction with the words and ideas put forth by your opponent. Even if you listened at Levels 2 and 3 and your opponent did *not*, it would result in a profound difference in how the two of you were perceived by the audience and further highlight your versatility and strength as the emotionally intelligent candidate.

What the Pros Know: Recover, Recover, Recover

Physically, how fit you are is determined by how quickly your body can recover from stress. One way to measure physical fitness is by how quickly your heartbeat recovers to its resting rate after exertion. In a study of high-performing tennis players, Jim Loehr and Tony Schwartz discovered that what separated the champions from those just below them was not so much level of skill (all the top players were *highly* skilled), but their ability to physically and emotionally recover, both during a game, and between games. How well they rested counted as much as how hard they trained. This gave them the energy they needed to play at their peak, game after game, throughout the match.

The ability to recover is invaluable to you as a leader. You will need to practice recovering constantly, moment to moment, and from one period to the next. When you've made a mistake, gone too far, or headed in the wrong direction, the sooner you return to a state of resourcefulness and power, the more adept you will be at responding to the next big challenge. You have a political agenda—ideas that you feel will make the world you live in more secure, just and prosperous. As you fight for this agenda, you will create alliances to support it, and counter any obstacles that block the way. You will be brilliant and right on point at times. At other times, you will be off-base or downright wrong. And it's likely you will fail at all three levels of listening. Regardless of whether your instincts are correct or not, what will set you apart from others will be exactly that which distinguishes champion athletes from the rest: your ability to recover quickly to a neutral position, gather yourself and be flexible, so you can create new initiatives and respond to existing ones with ease.

But *how* exactly do you recover? What should you do when you discover that you're in the wrong place or are out of step with what you believe? Return to the home of your strongest values. Leaders who maintain the ability to see and hold paradoxical points of view must be faithful to their personal values, which are reflected in their political philosophy. Imagine these personal and political values are a stake driven deeply into the ground. They clarify your priorities and guide you toward congruent policies and legislation. Holding to who you are and what you stand for, rather than reacting to public opinion, is easier said than done. It demands rigorous, introspective personal work—work for which having a coach can be very helpful.

A coach can help you to amplify the power of your leadership by showing you how to lead from a broader base of being: your emotional intelligence as well as your intellect. The more of yourself you bring to your leadership, the more your power and natural charisma increase. When you show up fully authentic, you model for others what powerful, full humanity looks like. And in doing this, you broadcast a profound respect for people and honor their inherent dignity.

In Conclusion

All of the great leaders have had one characteristic in common:
it was the willingness to confront unequivocally the major
anxiety of their people in their time. This, and not much else, is
the essence of leadership.
— John Kenneth Galbraith

One of the major anxieties of our time is whether we should have faith in our leaders. Can we trust you—our political leaders—to protect and inform us? Can we trust you to shepherd us toward a safe, prosperous, and sustainable future, where we will be more just with each other, more peaceful, and more united as a society than we are today?

As citizens, we are hungry for frankness and truth-telling, for information that is not first washed, filtered, and artfully arranged on a shiny platter for the media. We want our politicians to say, "I don't know" when they don't know and then offer, "but I'll do my best to find out and get back to you." We are hungry for emotional intelligence in our leaders. We want leaders whose commitment and resilience reminds us of our own power, and whose integrity aligns us with our own deepest values, with each other, and as a nation.

Lanny Davis, President Clinton's special counsel from 1996 to 1998, has written in his book *Truth to Tell: Tell It Early, Tell It All, Tell It Yourself,* that both sides of the aisle must be more honest. In an op-ed to the *New York Times* he wrote: "The best result of this latest scandal (the revealing of CIA agent Valerie Wilson's identity to the press) and the hypocrisy and finger-pointing exhibited on both sides, would be for voters to say, 'A pox on both your houses,' reject the scandal culture and gotcha politics of both parties, and see new politics of common cause, collegiality and the public interest."

In fact, the new politics would not be new at all. For millennia, long before the establishment of complex governmental systems, humans have sat together, talked and listened. We have talked about our hopes, our dreams, our fears, our victories and our failures. It is time to take a deep breath and pursue the game of politics from this perspective—from a place of authenticity, engaging with civility, absence of ego and true collegiality.

And so, anchored deeply to your values, go out there and engage in conversations. Be yourself—transparent and authentic. Tell the truth, and dare to recover publicly when you have made a mistake. Listen deeply and with great curiosity to the people you serve. And let the real conversation begin.

Samuel P. B. House, MCC
Soulutions Leadership and Consulting
518.475.7813 – *sam@soulutionsleadership.com*

Sam House, president of Soulutions Leadership and Consulting, is a Master Certified Coach and a leadership consultant. For over 20 years, he has engaged in bringing out the best in others in his roles as a coach, a leader/facilitator, and as a therapist. As a senior faculty member for the Coaches Training Institute—the largest coaching training organization in the world—Sam has worked with emerging leaders in the top Fortune 100 companies. He designs and delivers programs that result in high team effectiveness and full-permission leadership at all levels of an organization. In addition, he provides intensive and experientially based leadership training in northern California, Europe, and Asia for leaders across the globe.

Anne Long Fifield, CPCC
718.722.7571 – *anne@annefifield.com*

Anne Fifield is a Co-active Professional Certified Coach and an independent communications strategist. For more than 15 years, she has worked with leaders and entrepreneurs in media, advertising, finance, and technology. Anne is known for her creativity, her passionate commitment to clarity, and her ability to handle complicated situations and information in ways that promote rapport. She has been selected to work on complex and sensitive assignments with cultural and non-profit institutions such as The Pope John Paul II Cultural Center, the National Museum for Civil Rights, The Pioneer Institute, and the Military Academy at West Point.

A graduate of Princeton University, Anne has taught strategic communications at The City University of New York (CUNY). Her private coaching clients include accomplished solo artists, entrepreneurs, and competitive athletes.

The Paradox Potion:
Turning Politicians into Statesmen

Betsy Corley Pickren

Why is it that the word *politician* causes the American constituency to frown and the word *statesman* elicits a proud smile? *Politician* is defined (Wordweb.com, Princeton University) as "a leader engaged in civil administration, a person active in party politics, a schemer who tries to gain advantage in an organization in sly or underhanded ways." *Statesman* is defined as "a [person] who is a respected leader in national or international affairs." Quite a difference!

There is one catch, however. We recognize statesmen by looking backward at what they have accomplished and how they accomplished it. I envision the eventual emergence of *intentional statespeople* as our new political leaders. Right out of the starting gate, this new breed sets their sites on the goal of becoming well-known for courage, conviction and commitment to service, and they sidestep the selfish misuse of power. Now here's the challenge: How do we change the sequence and identify the potential of *intentional statespeople* when we first elect them instead of years later with 20/20 hindsight?

The biggest difference between the two is that statesmen have a magic potion that causes them to see, accept and use seemingly impossible or contradictory combinations of ideas and actions. I believe that political leaders emerge not through the consistent repetition of the same behaviors—using one color after another in a neat row—but through mixing colors that appear not to go together. It is this magic, masterful melting of inconsistencies in thinking and behavior—the ability to master paradoxical thinking—that turns politicians into statesmen.

For example, the issue of conservative and liberal thinking is neither a war to be won nor a problem to be solved. There is no right answer. It is a dilemma to be managed–a paradox. Behaving as if either side will win the other over is ludicrous. The underlying values of each side are too embedded, and there are kernels of wisdom in each. It will take the best thinking of both conservatives AND liberals to make headway on the complex issues of the 21st Century. How can we honor the brilliance in each viewpoint at the same time and get out of the trap of blaming and discounting? Imagine applying the strength of each side to the issue of dealing with poverty on our own shores and outward into the world. Imagine living in the tension of conflicting ideas for the purpose of taming terrorism in the world. Imagine painting a vision of the future of our planet with those contrasting colors. Only *intentional statespeople* will be able to craft such a progressive masterpiece.

The world, especially the USA, is ready for the ultimate reality series. It would go something like this: Politicians vie against each other to find the magic potion that turns them into *intentional statespeople.* Once the contestants drink this potion, POOF!, they turn into authentic leaders who compel citizens to crowd the polls to vote FOR them, not just AGAINST their opponents. And once the political leaders consume this concoction, there is no antidote. Oh, where is Harry Potter when we need him?

Beyond Magic

Here's another thought. What if magic potions are not the only way to grow this crop of new political leaders? Robert Louis Stevenson suggested that politics is perhaps the only profession for which no preparation is thought necessary. What would it take to change that paradigm?

I do my core coaching work in organizations. My ideal clients are leaders who can make a difference by gaining results while acting from their core values. When people reach management positions in the most successful organizations, they usually take advantage of professional development opportunities such as training, education and executive coaching. They get to know themselves first and then leverage that self-leadership into the ability to lead others. They relish being accountable for results while also behaving ethically.

Admittedly, some organizational leaders do not take those developmental opportunities seriously or, as they move up in the organization, they believe they have outgrown the need for leadership learning altogether. In their own opinions, they are infallible. The collapse of Enron and WorldCom are the results of leaders who exhibit that kind of pompousness. Those top leaders forgot that authentic leadership requires lifelong learning.

Making the News

Unfortunately, executives like those at Enron and WorldCom are the ones who make the news. We know the names of fallen business tycoons because they are blasted at us over television, on the radio and in newspaper headlines. To find the names of business leaders who quietly create value both in the bottom line and in the lives of employees, we have to WANT to find them and we need the time to search the web or the means to fork out $25 or more at the bookstore.

Similarly, it's also the dishonest politicians who make the news. We recognize the names of public officials who land in prison each year. We don't know as much about those politicians who do remember to keep learning, cling to their values and exhibit ethical behavior. Real leaders in the world of politics prepare for the tests embedded in every day of service, and they know that the public does not grade on the curve.

If you are already a politician, do you ever wake up in the middle of the night and think, "I wonder why so many people mistrust me when they don't even know me? Why does the public trust mythical TV Presidents Bartlett (of *The West Wing*) and Allen (of *Commander in Chief*), and over 60% (at this writing) don't trust President Bush?"

Have you also noticed that business leaders have it easy compared to politicos? It takes them much longer to get caught. As a public leader, you, on the other hand, make one misstep or one mistake and your face is immediately plastered all over the local and national news. Why? Because you are a politician and the public expects you to get it wrong.

Preparing, Practicing and Accepting Help

So the question arises: *What preparation is necessary for people to enter politics and, almost more important, to stay and grow in politics?*

Consider Tiger Woods. He prepared to be a professional golfer by learning and practicing golf as a child. He prepares for the next tournament by working with a coach and by studying his habits and choices. When Tiger engages in a tournament, he prepares for the next day; when he is playing, he prepares for the next stroke. And so it goes. To be world-class at anything, learning, self-examination and reviews of the basics can never stop. Tiger is both a master AND a learner.

With all due respect to Tiger, however, many more people feel the repercussions of the decisions made by a US President, senator, congressperson, governor, legislator, mayor or councilperson than by a decision about which golf club to use. Still, if you're a politician who wants to be an *intentional statesperson,* you must be willing to learn from the best of the best—in any field.

You can also learn from the worst. According to an article by Matt Apuzzo, Associated Press, published in *The Atlanta Journal-Constitution* on March 19, 2005:

> In December of 2004, former governor of Connecticut John Rowland pleaded guilty to a corruption charge, admitting that he sold his influence for more than $100,000 in trips to Las Vegas, vacations and improvements to his lakeside cottage. He resigned as the talk about impeachment became louder. He was fined and sentenced to three years' probation. According to an article from the Associated Press, Gov. Rowland told US District Judge Peter Dorsey, "I let my pride get in my way." And Rowland became one of more than a dozen former governors to be sent to prison.

Another quote from that article caught my attention. Federal prosecutor Nora Dannehy, in arguing for a longer sentence, told the judge: "Honest government matters. It has to matter. Send that message. Send it loud and clear. Without that rule of law, we are all lost." Amen.

I, for one, do not choose to be a part of a lost world. Instead, I am a critical member of the leadership team, supporting competent, honest, *intentional statespeople.* Building on the African proverb, maybe it takes a village to raise and support a competent representative in our government. Maybe that's why such "learning villages" are popping up here and there like stray daisies. Consider Ohio Executive Leadership Institute, Voinovich Center for Leadership and Public Affairs, and Camp Wellstone. Look at the Center for a Better South—a pragmatic, nonpartisan think tank dedicated to developing progressive ideas, policies and information for thinking leaders who want to make a difference in the American South.

Internationally, there are organizations like the Romanian nongovernmental organization that organizes nonpartisan workshops for young political leaders, and the program launched in Pakistan for the education and training in political processes of female leaders and representatives of local bodies across the country.

Executive coaches add to the village of support. Coaches and clients partner for the primary purpose of moving clients toward their visions of excellence. The original meaning of the word coach in English was a particular kind of carriage that conveyed highly-regarded people from where they were to where they wanted to be. When a professional coach and a visionary political leader join forces, that leader is more likely to reach the desired destination of becoming a statesman.

Perspectives on Challenges Our Political Leaders Face

In his book, *Polarity Management: Identifying and Managing Unsolvable Problems,* Dr. Barry Johnson says that, while there are problems to solve, there are also many issues that are not solvable. We drive ourselves crazy in our efforts to tie a bow around them and label them "fixed." And then we feign surprise when they arise again.

Craig A. Rimmerman, series editor of "Dilemmas in American Politics," says:

> If the answers to the problems facing American democracy were easy, politicians would solve them, accept credit and move on. But certain dilemmas have confronted the American political system continuously. They defy solution; they are endemic to the system.

He goes on to identify a few problems, such as: How do we compromise on issues that defy compromise, like abortion laws? How do we welcome and incorporate ethnic and racial minorities into American society so they reap benefits but don't lose their own culture?

When faced with dilemmas like these, our representatives are forced to call on what Jim Collins and Jerry Porras describe in their book, *Built to Last,* as "the genius of the AND." The authors dispute such proclamations as:

> You can have low cost OR high quality.
> You can have change OR stability.
> You must be conservative OR liberal.

Built to Last is written about corporations, but don't we have a vision of American democratic governance as one that is built to last forever?

In *God's Politics: Why the Right Gets it Wrong and the Left Doesn't Get It*, Jim Wallis puts forth a new vision for faith and politics in America. In one chapter, he tackles the issue of poverty in our country. He takes the media to task for sniffing out only stories with conflict. Many talk-show hosts choose people to interview who have the most radical opposing views to make the conversation (if you can call it that) lively. They perpetuate the OR mentality. They ignore the possibility that complex social issues require looking at a number of perspectives rather than stuffing comments neatly into one side or the other. In reality, neither side has the solution.

Wallis says:

> To be disciplined by results requires us to be less concerned about ideological presuppositions and more focused on what actually works. What is liberal OR conservative would be replaced by what's right and what works. It is a solution-based approach to overcoming poverty, not a blame-based debate. Instead of just pointing fingers and blaming the other side, we focus together on finding solutions that really work.

Poverty is one of the complex issues facing politicians at every level of government. To bring that to mind, we only have to remember the recent Katrina catastrophe. TVs, radios and newspapers magnified the picture of poverty in the Southern states. For once, we could not cram our own problems behind the sofa. We were not taking care of our own and the whole world witnessed it. Who is to blame? Is it the city government? The state government? The national government? The liberals? The conservatives? Or all of us? The bigger question is: Who is responsible for taking steps to ensure that the problems we faced in Louisiana, Mississippi and Alabama do not repeat themselves?

If our politicians aspire to wrestle with mammoth dilemmas like poverty and come out winners, they must drink the magic potion, then reach deep within themselves and pull out their paradoxical strengths. They must become *intentional statespeople*.

In another chapter in this book, I ask, "What is an authentic leader?" The dialogue forced by that question is important. One possibility is that authentic leaders and *intentional statespeople* are aware of paradoxical forces at work in the world and within themselves. They embrace the complexity of themselves as a whole person rather than trying to create a one-dimensional persona. They recognize that people have the capacity to be emotional and analytical in solving problems. It is possible to be a visionary who get things done.

I am not advocating that we look for perfection in our politicians. As long as our only options are mere mortals, we will encounter flaws and inauthentic behaviors. We will be disappointed that they don't live up to our expectations. What I am advocating is that, as an electorate, we choose political leaders whose intention is to move toward authenticity in their campaigns and in their official positions—*intentional statespeople*. Because of the complexity of such a challenge, ongoing learning in the form of coaching can be a major contributor to this new breed of politicos who operate from their paradoxical strengths in dealing with the dilemmas of our time.

Examples of Paradox in Political Leadership

I invite you to suspend judgment and think with me for the duration of this chapter about having leaders who do indeed harness the power of paradox by invoking the genius of "AND." How would that ability to consciously bring together two seemingly contradictory sides of oneself, or of an issue, to achieve outstanding results make a positive difference? It is possible.

In May 2005, a group of senators, now known as "the gang of 14" got together. Seven Republicans agreed not to vote to eliminate the filibuster for judicial nominations, and the seven Democrats agreed to filibuster only in "extreme circumstances." In a polarized political environment, the centrists got together and worked it out. Each of them discovered the power of "AND" … if only briefly.

Take a look back at the two candidates we had before us in the presidential election of 2004. The voters were given a choice between two extremes. The media and the two major parties reinforced this picture of the candidates' brains regarding "the war on terror." Gary Markstein says it best in his cartoon.

Reprinted with permission from Copley News Service

So there we were at the polls with a choice between a flip-flopper and a pighead. Not very exciting. Most of us went to vote AGAINST one or the other. What we really craved was a person who would stand strong in the belief that ongoing dialogue with world leaders will build coalitions that will, in the long run, bind us together to destroy the few who choose to terrorize AND, one who would take decisive action immediately when warranted. We wanted collaboration AND authoritarian decision making. We wanted someone who could listen and take in new information, was open and reflective, AND was certain that his own opinion was built on solid evidence. Someone who could blend two sides into wisdom. *An intentional statesperson.*

The challenge for politicians is to be aware of their own core paradoxes and stay in the upsides of their character traits rather than letting the public's perception of the downsides win out. Using the Harrison Assessment tool, let's review Markstein's Kerry-Bush example and examine two traits that combine to create paradoxical leadership strength:

AUTHORITATIVE: The desire for decision-making authority and the willingness to accept decision-making responsibility.

COLLABORATIVE: The tendency to pull others together when making decisions.

A descriptive proverb for this paradox might be: "Take counsel from appropriate people AND yet always take full responsibility for your own decisions."

Dan Harrison is the author of *Harrison Assessment*, which incorporates paradox theory as a philosophy. His premise is that paradoxical forces can be applied to the human psyche as well as to organizational or governmental dynamics. I think paradox theory has huge implications for how we choose our political leaders, as well as how they lead once they are in office.

The Harrison Assessment tool helps translate the possible combinations of two paradoxical traits into "behavior buckets" called:

- **Versatile behavior**
- **Aggressive behavior**
- **Passive behavior**
- **Deficient behavior**

Four applications for the paradox of Authoritative and Collaborative:

AGGRESSIVE: Authoritarian—The tendency to make decisions without consulting with others (high Authoritative and low Collaborative).	VERSATILE: Authoritative Collaboration—The tendency to take responsibility for decisions, while at the same time allowing others to genuinely participate in the decision-making process (high Authoritative and high Collaborative).
DEFICIENT: Avoids Decisions—The tendency to avoid decision-making authority, while at the same time avoiding making decisions jointly with others (low Authoritative and low Collaborative).	PASSIVE: Defers Decisions—The tendency to avoid making decisions by referring them to others (low Authoritative and high Collaborative).

Other examples of leadership paradoxes include:
- Assertive AND helpful
- Enforcing rules AND warmth and empathy
- Frankness AND diplomacy
- Risking AND analyzing pitfalls
- Being certain about opinions AND being open to others' opinions

The Versatile "bucket" is the one that defines the strength of operating in both areas at the same time. During the 2004 presidential election, the powerful question for each candidate would have been, "How do you intend to combine collaboration with other countries AND responsible decision making as you lead the world in fighting terrorism?"

There are many examples of successful leaders who blend seemingly opposite traits. The prescript is that both sides of the paradoxical behaviors must be authentic for the paradoxes to be strengths. Characteristics that most people label as negative or wrong are simply an extreme form of qualities that can be positive and right when used well. In *Paradoxical Thinking: How to Profit from your Contradictions,* Jerry Fletcher and Kelle Olwyler cite two political examples, President Bill Clinton and Governor Mario Cuomo.

According to biographer David Maraniss, Bill Clinton can be both sincere and calculating at the same time without either side being false. Maybe this authentic paradox played a part in the segment of his career that has made a positive difference as well as in the segment that brought down his presidency. There IS an upside to both of these traits. Another way to put it is that he wants to help others get what they want in life; he does care about meeting their needs. And, at the same time, he intends to get what he needs. To operate in the up sides of both of those perspectives at the same time requires a mastery of paradox, and the result is true power. Does Clinton possess the ingredients to concoct the magic potion? Will history view him as an *intentional statesman*?

TIME magazine opened a cover story about Mario Cuomo's possible run for President with a description of him ending in this quote:

> Mario Matthew Cuomo, the governor of New York, is both of these men: the man of strenuous action and the man of otherworldly contemplation.

It is a mistake to think of Cuomo as solely the passionate, strong and action-oriented man, or to assume that he is only intellectual, ascetic and reflective. Both sides are authentic. He combined those two sides well enough to win the governorship of New York for three four-year terms. He could understand and deal with the demands of diverse interests groups and also implement his great ideas.

In late 1966, I worked on Zell Miller's campaign for Congress in the 9th District of Georgia. One day a woman came to the campaign office and, as I remember, identified herself as the secretary of the Georgia Senate. At the time, a senator, who was also a peanut farmer, was running for governor of Georgia. "I like Jimmy Carter," my teenaged self said. "Can he win?"

"No," the woman said. "He is much too honest."

Can a political leader be too honest? Is there a downside to honesty? When does honesty become a liability? Some people see "honest politician" as the ultimate oxymoron. All I know is that the woman was right. Carter didn't win that election. But he was elected governor of Georgia in 1971 and President in 1976.

What changed? Did Carter stop being honest? I don't believe that's the case. So what was the seemingly contradictory trait that Jimmy Carter embraced that allowed him to become governor and eventually President of the United States? The paradoxical trait could have been "willingness to compromise in service of a higher goal." The question merits thought. *Honest* is still an adjective most people would use to describe the former President; therefore, I conclude that he added another dimension. Perhaps he became more cunning and calculating so he could get what he wanted—the chance to be of service to the world.

Throughout his political career, Zell Miller has been a master at handling paradoxical traits—taking risks and analyzing pitfalls, and being both frank and respectful. I had always seen him as either a gentle tyrant or tyrannical gentleman—sometimes his behavior spiked more on one side or the other—but at the end of those days, he did not wallow in the downside of either.

Unfortunately, it was these same traits that got him in trouble with many of his political base. How? He sank into the downside of both traits by forgetting diplomacy, respect, civility and gratitude. The culmination came during his speech at the Republican convention of 2004 in which he accused Democrats of "being motivated more by partisan politics than national security." He also said that the Democrats were wrong when "they" choose the "pacifism" of Carter. As most people clearly remembered, Miller had proudly used the pronoun "we" in 1976 when advocating Carter for President. And when he launched his attack on John Kerry, many of us lost the meaning of his words in the anger of them. As an American, I believe that people can be *for* something AND be civil to the people who have a different opinion—especially when those people elected them. That's the statesman way. In the same speech, Senator Miller also asked, "Where are such statesmen today? Where is the bipartisanship in this country when we need it the most?" Indeed, those are the right questions.

Now let's consider President George W. Bush. Once a highly popular President, his ratings are low in the polls these days. He may be operating in the downside of some paradoxes. In a 2001 *Harvard Business Review* article, "Level 5 Leadership: The Triumph of Humility and Fierce Resolve," Jim Collins describes the yin and yang that top leaders master: personal humility and professional will. Here are some qualities that a paradoxically positive leader displays:

Personal Humility	Professional Will
Demonstrates a compelling modesty, shunning public adulation; never boastful.	Creates superb results; a clear catalyst in the transition from good to great.
Acts with quiet, calm determination; relies principally on inspired standards, not inspiring charisma, to motivate.	Demonstrates an unwavering resolve to do whatever must be done to produce the best long-term results, no matter how difficult.
Looks in the mirror, not out the window, to apportion responsibility for poor results, never blaming other people, external factors or bad luck.	Looks out the window, not in the mirror, to apportion credit for the success [of the endeavor or company] to other people, external factors and good luck.

How has President Bush lived in the tension between personal humility and professional will? You decide. Consider other politicians as well—pick one—how do they manage the Level 5 leadership paradox? These are the questions I would like to see us raise. Inspired, respectful dialogue and thoughtful examination of today's elected officials will lead us to discover answers to the challenges of political leadership. Together, as citizens of the world, we can create a future that is worthy of the best we have to offer.

Taking the Steps with a Coach

I believe the following actions will help you, as a politician, become an *intentional statesman:*

1. Recognize the paradoxes.

Recognize the criticality of both sides and stop arguing for the "either/or." Be intentional. Be ruthless about holding yourself accountable for the whole picture of strength, not just part of it. Being decisive is positive. Involving others in decision-making is positive. Each behavior is right—just incomplete on its own. Contract with your coach to help you discover the "AND."

2. Be sensitive to the downsides as they are experienced by you and others.

How do you recognize the other side of the paradox? By being aware of perceptions. Consider what actions make you most uncomfortable so you can hone in on the downside of the companion paradoxical trait and avoid it. What is it that you absolutely do NOT want others to say about you? Ask your coach to challenge you to stretch in the direction that is most uncomfortable for you.

3. Notice when something is not working.

Imagine that one of your legs is shorter than the other. Naturally, you would put more weight on the longer leg and tend to limp to that side. As that leg gets stronger, you intentionally favor that side of the body. After awhile, it becomes too frightening to put more weight on the shorter leg—you might fall down. Never mind that your entire spine is out of alignment and the health of your body is being adversely affected. You just continue to do what is most comfortable rather than what will create the most overall good. If you're leaning toward the downside, it's hard to learn to stand straight again. Your coach can hold up a mirror so that you can check your alignment.

4. Demonstrate a willingness to shift sides—to increase your range of behavior.

Ask for help. Bring in a behavioral chiropractor—a coach—to assist in the adjustment. Spend time contemplating the other side. Pay attention to it. Get out of your comfort zone and try behaviors that are not as easy. Go though the pain and discomfort of using the shorter leg, and allow yourself to take a risk with eyes wide open and pitfalls identified. Really look at the consequences of relying too heavily on the stronger side. You may find that, despite your anxiety, you actually walk faster and reach your goal more easily.

5. If the range of behavior is too difficult to maintain, create strategies or structures that assure that your weaker trait gets exercised in some way.

Your body may not be capable of maintaining the versatility that a balanced strength requires. If so, outside resources can make the difference. For example, a shoe lift will bring the legs into balance. A coach or trusted advisor might play the role of the weaker side to make sure it gets a voice. Rely on tools or checklists. Make a commitment to try a new behavior at least once a day. For example, if you are used to making decisions alone and announcing them, put one meeting per day on your calendar for the purpose of soliciting and listening to someone else's opinion before you make that final decision. A coach can hold you accountable for actually carrying out the new behavior.

6. Notice the positive impact your magnified competency has on others and on your goal of creating beneficial permanence by meeting the real needs of the people you serve.

Reflection rules. Just ask yourself and your colleagues and your adversaries and your constituents. Analyze your performance and adjust—constantly. Find a method of reflection with a coach, a journal, meditation or something else.

Like the most effective organizational leaders, the most effective political leaders recognize the complexity of issues. To do so, you must be an *intentional statesperson*, work to increase the ranks of other *intentional statespeople*, doggedly embrace the power of the "AND", honor the fullness of your own paradoxical strengths, and call forth those strengths in your supporters and your adversaries in service of common goals. Turn Robert Louis Stevenson's quote around to read, *For me, the profession of politics demands* constant *preparation, reflection and awareness.*

Apply the Insight
Harnessing the power of paradox

1. Recognize the paradoxes.
2. Be sensitive to the downsides as they are experienced by you and others.
3. Notice when something is not working.
4. Demonstrate a willingness to shift sides—to increase your range of behavior.
5. If the range of behavior is too difficult to maintain, create strategies or structures that assure that your weaker trait gets exercised in some way.
6. Notice the positive impact your magnified competency has on others and on your goal of becoming an intentional statesman.

The Body Politic:
Political Leadership Integrity Model

Dennis S. Brogan

The body politic (the aggregate people of a politically organized nation or state) constantly evolves, challenges and changes. The center of the body is always in motion. So where is the center today, and why?

In this modern age of politics, where communication travels at the speed of light, the body politic must be centered in integrity. If there is a perceptual, or even real, challenge in politics with integrity, it is not the media's fault, although everyone on both political fringes yells, "The media is ruining politics today." No, it's our fault—all of ours. Keeping integrity at our center is the biggest challenge for the body politic. Without integrity, we can't make the right decisions as voters, as politicians, as staff and support people, as members of the media covering the race, or as candidates.

What is integrity?

Integrity is defined as "The firm adherence to a code or standard of values; the state of being unimpaired; soundness." At the center of the word *integrity* lays the word *grit*. *Grit* epitomizes the faith, courage, strength and will to hold the course on the things around us that challenge our values. *Having grit* means taking a stand for personal beliefs in the face of adversity, challenges and opposition.

By definition, *grit* is "indomitable spirit." A person has *true grit* when others recognize that quality and rely on that person to stand for and with them. Hence, when we are in integrity, we are living our grit. Most baby boomers can envision John Wayne as Rooster Cogburn riding against the herd of thieves, murderers and rapists in the movie *True Grit*, the reins of his horse in his teeth, guns blazing, defending a young woman and her family's honor—living his grit.

How Do You Find Your Grit?

In the movie *Rob Roy*, starring Liam Neesom, there is a scene in which Neesom's son asks his chieftain father, "What does it mean to give someone your word?" The father answers, "Your word is something that no man can take, and only you can give away." Did you get that? No one can take away another's integrity—not the media, not a political consultant, not family, not friends. Only the individual holds the responsibility for living with integrity and demonstrating true grit.

Is that true for political leaders? You bet it is! Whether they are elected officials or one of the many other political leaders with careers in government, political people are pulled from every angle. From family to community to politics to law, there is always some issue pulling at their political soul.

Whether it's a local election for commissioner or a major regional, state or federal position, the body politic is pulled from four distinct areas that form the Political Leadership Integrity Model (PLIM).

PLIM contains four elementary components that can work in partnership or in conflict. They are family, law, community and politics. These areas of integrity are unique to themselves, and the candidate or politician may be in one area at this moment and in another area 15 minutes from now. The ideal place to be plotted with the elements of the PLIM is dead center. The moment and topicality of each component can change in a flash because of something on the Internet or a story on the news. Political leaders must always be aware of their surroundings in order to manage the moment, the opportunities and their integrity centers. Integrity shows up in and by the moment.

Questions to consider:
- How does a political leader, staffer or executive coach use PLIM?
- How do you know where you are centered in each area? Why is it important?
- Where do the media outlets see you in regard to your integrity?
- How do the public and your constituents perceive your integrity?
- Where do your political friends and foes see you in this model?
- Where might your staff or peers place you in the model?
- How about your competitors? Where do they place you?
- How often do you check your integrity center?

I believe you can use the Political Leadership Integrity Model to support yourself as a leader, to assist your staff or peers in advancing their leadership goals, and to advance democracy in our towns, villages, counties, parishes, cities, states and nation. Remember that all politics are local, and today the whole globe is becoming local.

Family

Think of the many times you have seen this on television: The candidate stands with their family on stage, all with huge victorious smiles, after winning their race on election night. Accepting a victory is easy, for winning is exhilarating. Excitement and joy fill the air. But every elected official at some point will face an integrity issue—real or perceived. And that issue may challenge their individual body politic.

The lifecycle of a person in politics is 24 hours. In those 24 hours, there are 1,440 minutes, which supports the concept of Politics at the Speed of Light. Those 24 hours often start with the delivery of the morning paper. You see a headline about your loss of integrity, or at least a challenge to it. The web, newspaper or other forums bring innuendo and unsourced accusations that can multiply by the second. If you are a public leader who must make decisions, your and your family's integrity will always be a moment away from scrutiny. If our democratic system is in need of repair, our own integrity is the place to begin.

You can see the results regularly. The New Jersey governor is a good example. He was forced to resign because of a relationship with, and the subsequent hiring of, an individual who may not have been qualified for the position. The governor had to apologize to his wife, the community and the people for his error in judgment and his indiscretion. As he did so, his wife stood tall by his side. The family is always there and often, like in business, the candidate is pulled away from being in integrity with the family at that moment.

"Family" includes your spouse, life partner, children, grandchildren, aunts, uncles and friends. These are the people who will usually be there for you with unquestioned loyalty and dedication. Your families are the individuals who pick you up when you're down and stand by your side when the world seems to be turning on you. But you alone will still have to answer questions about the integrity issues.

- How do you establish whether you are out of integrity with your family?
- How do you get centered in integrity with your family?
- How can your family support you in this area?
- How can you support them?

The answer to the second question is to ask yourself where you are plotted in the family quadrant of the PLIM.
- Are you near the center?
- Which is the ideal position?
- Are you so far from the center that you are near the edge?

Now the hard part: You must ask those in your immediate family if they have observed any challenges, issues or behavior where integrity may be an issue. The family's observations are often the best indicator of a person's integrity and intent. In other words, they know first if you are heading out of the integrity center. Coaching will also support you in finding the family integrity center by making sure you are "being your word."

Law

The law is spelled out in black and white words, and the words should be reflected in the political person's actions. Whether you are required to take an oath of office or are appointed to support an elected official, you give your word to uphold the law, sometimes with one hand on the Bible and the other raised in support of the oath. It is a splendid moment when a person takes the oath of office and swears to uphold the Constitution of the United States of America, to uphold their state Constitution, to uphold the charter of their city, county, village or town. You swear it for the people and you swear it before God.

The words of law may be printed in black and white, but the interpretation and intent of those words lie in the way you read them—the way you or a staffer understands the enormous task of being your word. Remember that people see you in living color.

If I were your executive coach, I might ask you these questions, so I urge you to ask them of yourself:

- "Is there any area of the law or your oath that might interfere with your ability to make a decision?" I am not assuming that there *is* an integrity issue. I ask this question to help you support others in a way that no one else likely will.
- "Is there any person or group around you that is challenging your integrity with the law or your oath?" Political people are often presented with a question or situation that can be near the line. A staffer could have an integrity issue that may infect their boss or client. A special interest group could be pressuring staffers or leaders to

make a favorable decision because the business or industry supported their campaign. If there are concerns in this area, your support from a coach can be crucial in getting centered.

- "Are you concerned about the people you are surrounded by?" These people may be in your world by circumstance, not by choice. Private life is much different from public life. Politicians are usually judged by the company they keep.
- "If you were to describe the ideal outcome from your efforts, what would it look like?" Create movement that leads to discovery.

Community

The community is your customer base. These are the folks who elect you to office. Or don't elect you, or are so disillusioned with the system that they don't vote at all. It's the neighborhood watch groups, homeowners' associations, ethnic groups, business leaders, educators, religious organizations, and a host of other special interest groups and individuals who want to be heard.

Your constituents read the newspaper, listen to the news, scan local and/or national publications, and get information on the Internet. Constituent customers get their information in 12-second sound bites from blogs, and they hear the water-cooler chat that is influenced by all of these factors and more. Hence my earlier statement that we in the political arena live by a 24-hour life cycle. What is even more challenging is that people aren't really as informed as in the past; the public makes their decisions for the most part by emotion and not values. The conflict between emotion and values is real. Our emotions are influenced by wanting and needing approval, gratification, acknowledgment and ego strokes.

I often ask myself as a coach how I can best support political leaders in this area. The answer is really quite simple: through listening, thinking and coaching them on how to better connect with their constituent customers. In the business of political leading, much like in the private sector, the leader does not want customers who are satisfied—they want customers who are *more than* satisfied. The coach supports political leadership by asking how they might better communicate one-to-one with people. My goal is supporting them so their constituent customers are more than satisfied with their work, their standards, their problem-solving ability, and ultimately, their leadership. The leader's ability to model *generous listening* while hearing their constituent customers' concerns, ideas and challenges is essential. They must understand these basic communication strengths, and it is my job to support them in doing so.

In the community triangle, it is essential that you look at your constituents as customers, not taxpayers. Shifting your language can redirect the way the constituent customer connects with you. Another area for positively supporting your constituent customers is community partnerships. As a coach, I ask political leaders what areas of community they are strongest in, as well as what areas are their weakest. Understanding this will provide strength to the leaders, since at times they are acting as coach to a community. Hence it is important that a political leader understand how to manage partnering conversations, how to bridge conversations, and how to move forward as a coach might do with a client.

The Entrepreneurial Conversation, by Edward Rogoff and Michael Corbett with Perry-Lynn Moffitt, discusses the components of good conversations from an entrepreneurial point of reference. They ask readers to seek out the *real issues* of the game: to listen, think and speak. For leaders, it is essential to understand this concept, and think before speaking or asking a question. People often admire silence in a leader. It indicates listening to the real words and issues that are being voiced. Finally, leaders must speak in a way that other can hear them. For it is only the leaders themselves who are responsible for how they are heard.

Over the last decade, Rogoff and Corbett have separated conversations into four categories:

Circular Conversation, which consists of stories, gossip, complaints, negative thought, judgments, excuses and any other type of conversation that is not going anywhere.

Conversation for Possibilities, which consists of probing wonderment, questions, and a demonstrated interest in the person speaking that offers no judgment. This is where we "get" the other person and they begin to see that we are getting them.

Conversation for Action, which is the who, the what, and the by when. In the coaching conversation, this is when we reflect to the person speaking what we have heard them say. When we really hear someone, we can take the required steps to meet the expectations by our actions.

Conversation for Opportunity, in which the leader asks, "What is in it for me?" but does not make it the primary focus. The conversation is about the other person in the conversation. On a community level, the opportunity issue is in the eye of the beholder: One person's opportunity may be another's loss or win. How you use the opportunity conversation and the way you handle opportunity will most likely determine how you are judged by the community.

I must stress again that it is others' *real issues* that matter. If they believe you understand them, the world opens up for everyone involved.

In *The Power of Partnerships,* Riane Eisler writes about the Domination Model. In this model, one party dominates the other to influence the outcome. In the Partnership Model, both parties work to ensure that each receives the benefit of the agreement and one does not outweigh the other. It is essential to understand the difference. Dr. Eisler references over 30,000 years of history that show we never reach our potential under the Domination Model. And that men, women and children thrive under the Partnership Model.

Politics

This fourth area of the PLIM is the most difficult for the public and political leaders alike. As a coach who also works in the political business, I am well aware of this. The politics of politics is where the strongest and fiercest pressures will come for leaders and the decisions you must make. These decisions will be influenced by party politics, business politics, neighborhood politics, family politics and office politics. The games people play will challenge your every decision. From the political position, we in public service are under the eye of the three other quadrants when we deal with the political integrity of politics.

I believe that when people enter public service, whether elected, appointed or inherited, we enter for the greater good of something bigger than us as individuals. In many cases, we enter because of a calling, a value someone transferred to us, or an emotional influence that drew us. Once in public service, we learn that our values, beliefs and integrity can be challenged every day. This challenge is no different from the private sector, except that we work for, and serve, the people. In public service, we work from a place of trust that the constituent customer expects, that *we* expect, and one that will always be challenged.

For that reason, in dealing with the "political being" inside all who serve, it will be our courage in moments of adversity, our depth of character when someone says or challenges our word or being, the strength of our vision to see through the fog of special interests, and our ability to generously hear the words around us that will provide the greater support in this area.

The challenges in this quadrant are many. The foes and pressures will be both public and private, and they will always be present. Most importantly, your ability to stay centered in all four areas will support you and the world around you to reach places greater than you may have thought possible.

The ability to lead, to be coached, and to provide modeling, mentoring and coaching to those in your community whom you support makes the political game and the body of politics reach beyond what most see possible today.

How to Use the PLIM to Find Your "Best Self Center"

The Political Leadership Integrity Model will help you make sure you are in your "best self center." We are swayed by both negative and positive influences that either pull us away from our best self center or draw us back to center everyday. Here are five easy steps to utilize for checking where you may be plotted on the PLIM and assist in identifying the Negative Influences (NI) and Positive Influences (PI) that challenge your "political being" everyday. By identifying them you can address them.

1. List up to five Negative Influences for each quadrant of the PLIM. These are symbolized by the NI Arrow pulling you away from the center.

2. List up to five Positive Influences for each quadrant of the PLIM. These are symbolized by the PI Arrow drawing you back to center.

3. Now that you have identified the influences in each quadrant choose one Negative Influence from each and identify if there is a Positive Influence you can use to overcome the Negative Influence. What personal value or personal integrity strength will support you in shifting from the negative force to the positive force? Hence using the positive to draw yourself back to the "Best Self Center,"

4. Identify the area of the PLIM has the most Negative Influences.

5. Identify the area of the PLIM has the most Positive Influence.

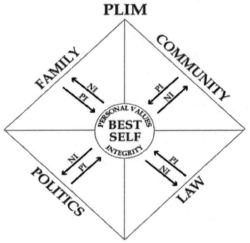

Key: NI = Negative Influences PI = Positive Influences
© *November 2005, WINS Coaching Services*

Now work through each NI and see how you can change it, shift it, or relinquish its influence over you, its shadow over those who you engage in this quadrant. Who can support you in this exercise and most importantly the moving back to center?

When you have finished this task move to the PI's and identify how you can use this strength to bring you to center and keep you there.

Now look at how you surround yourself with each Positive Influence. You should feel the strength of the positive overcoming the negative. This feeling is empowering and provides energy, rather than the loss of energy the negative succumbs to. An Executive Coach is a powerful support for you to ensure you are centered and have the supports for centering yourself.

Dennis S. Brogan
WINS Coaching Services
Syracuse, New York
315.382.4437
dennisb.newtonproducts@gmail.com

Dennis Brogan is a journeyman in business and service. He worked in broadcast radio as a morning radio cohost, sales executive and senior manager for nearly 20 years. His varied leadership roles include director of sales and development for Ryan Communications, a role where he oversaw an annual marketing and advertising budget of over $8 million dollars for Carrier Corporation's Enterprise Division. Dennis currently works at the executive level of local government as a senior staff member to Matthew J. Driscoll, mayor of the City of Syracuse.

A successful entrepreneur, Dennis also operates WINS Coaching Services, a business management, leadership and coaching service. His work includes coaching political and governmental leaders. Dennis is a member of the International Coach Federation.
In 2005, he started Newton Business Programs with Edward Rogoff, PhD. Newton Business Programs designs and delivers training and inspirational and communications programs for a variety of clients to support their growth and development. Dennis is also a commissioner of human rights in Syracuse, New York; a founding board member of the Syracuse International Film and Video Festival, the founding president of Rebuilding Together with Christmas in April in Syracuse and Binghamton, New York; a trustee of the Landmark Theater, and president and CEO of Good Karma Koffee Company and Importing.

Dennis has two beautiful daughters, Colleen and Meghan, to whom his contribution to this book is dedicated. Dennis is an avid outdoorsman, sailor and woodworker.

SERVE™: Strategic Communication

Erika Gabaldon

Strategic communication is what allows you, as public servants, to work well together. What is more, how you engage each other impacts your constituents, as well as listeners on a national and even global level. Strong communication skills are the most important tool you have when you work to provide for the well-being of your communities. As Cicero so succinctly put it, "The most successful politician is he who says loudest, and most frequently, what the people are thinking." While some may cynically view this statement as a sad commentary on politics, or as pandering to the masses, you mustn't forget that your very ability to know the people's needs, and thereby paint a compelling vision for change, will be the yardstick of your success in public life. Having the ability to communicate well is the difference between high achievement and political obscurity.

There is a customized communication protocol developed specifically for public servants who seek to maximize their ability to convey and synthesize public ideas. It's called SERVE™. SERVE™ provides you a set of communication values—a code of political communication that you can work with and rely on in every political situation. The guidelines established by SERVE™ are derived largely from the "Standards of Presence," which have been used successfully for more than 10 years in corporations, not-for-profits, graduate courses, universities, public schools, churches, and even a privately-run prison. Just six months after prison managers incorporated use of the Standards of Presence, employees reported that their supervisors listened 72% more effectively. The Standards of Presence are a valuable resource that I use extensively in my coaching practice. I saw how clients working in public realms could benefit from a set of values that spoke specifically to how they could better navigate the always-complicated (and often difficult) governmental and political communication. After extensive observations of public servants' communications styles, and their successes and failures, I adapted the Standards of Presence model to fit the rigorous and rapidly changing demands of a political landscape. SERVE™ was then born.

This chapter offers you ten ways to consciously make use of the SERVE™ values so you can artfully and authentically serve yourself and others.

SERVE™: A Code for Political Communication

SERVE™ offers you five communication values to draw from in all your interactions with colleagues and constituents. A basic premise of SERVE™ is that you first "own" these values and then take responsibility for them in your working relationships with others. In this section, I describe the five SERVE™ values and how they enhance your communication process. Then I will explore how, on your own or with a friend, colleague or executive coach, you can take ownership of, and responsibility for, these values when you communicate with others.

The core components of SERVE™ are: Security, Empowerment, Respect, View and Engagement.

Security:

Good communication develops from a safe and secure environment. When we feel secure, we are more able to let go of preconceived notions and judgments. We more readily accept ourselves, the others around us, and the situation before us. It engenders a sense of safety, so everyone can speak openly and honestly.

Empowerment:

When we feel empowered, we can confidently initiate communication. It begins by asking the question, "What do you know?" It is answered when you claim your authority and use it to advance shared goals. Also, be aware of what others know, and acknowledge their authority. Good communication arises when everyone has power and feels able to use it in a cooperative manner.

Respect:

Accept yourself, accept others, accept all beliefs and opinions. This does not demand that you adopt them as your own, but it does demand that you recognize the authenticity of those ideas without feeling threatened by them. Good communication results when we speak not to an *idea*, a perspective or a past experience, but to another *person*. When we respect others, we can also use our conversations to better our relationships with them.

View:

Be aware of your mind's attitude. Good communication is possible when we are open to many points of view rather than having just one "view." An open mind and a willingness to learn allow your ego to take a back seat so you can allow the common good to take priority. Don't confuse having a "view" with creating a "vision." Vision can give you purpose and direction but, when you are interacting with others, your vision becomes just one more view in the room.

Engagement:

Be fully present in mind, body and spirit. Good communication involves helping others to genuinely feel heard. When we give them our full attention, we demonstrate our experience of them. Also, when we are fully present, we are more able to focus on (and stay with) the communication moment and less likely to experience distractions.

How You SERVE™ Is Unique to You

SERVE™ offers you a set of values. To use these values, you'll need to understand what they mean to you and how you'd like to apply them. SERVE™ doesn't offer a "one value fits all" approach; the values are constant, but how you know them and want to work with them is unique to you. That's why talking about SERVE™ with a friend or colleague can be beneficial. Reflecting on these values with someone you trust will allow you to engage them more deeply. Listening to someone repeat what you shared will allow you to gauge the authenticity of your own responses. Owning these values will make you more credible. Others will see that how you communicate arises from who you really are.

Here are some questions to help you discover how you want to apply the SERVE™ values:

- How can you take charge of your own security? How can you be more self-accepting?

- How can you empower yourself? Are you assured in your ability? Do you trust yourself? Are you willing to accept a leadership role?

- Do you respect who you are and what you have to offer? Do you value your beliefs? Are you prepared to honestly and respectfully give and receive feedback?

- Do you have a "view"? Can you articulate it? What personal beliefs support your view? Honestly, how do you feel about others' views?

- Are you fully present and engaged? Are you aware of your surroundings? How do your words and actions demonstrate your commitment to serving the common good? Do you have a strategy for moving conversations forward? Are you willing to take action now?

SERVE™ asks you to take responsibility for your relationships with others. This will enable you to create a working environment where genuine communication can take place.

- What can you do to help others feel secure and accepted?

- How can you empower others to accomplish the work that needs to get done?

- How can you demonstrate respect for others' beliefs, accomplishments and power? How can you exhibit your desire to achieve results with them?

- How can you invite others to share your vision?
- How can you engage others' commitment to serving the community?

The more you embrace and make use of each SERVE™ value, the more effectively you'll communicate. When you allow SERVE™ to direct how you communicate with others, you provide a powerful example that inspires them to do the same.

Tone as well as Talk

At the close of the Second World War, Republican senator Arthur Vandenberg was known as a strong isolationist in the US Senate. But in 1945, he tantalized America (and his Democratic colleagues) with a speech that, among other things, marked an abrupt about-face in his prior philosophy, by declaring that the United States should participate in "collective security."

"…Somebody had to say something," Vandenberg said, "…It could be more effectively said by a member of the opposition." The effectiveness of Vandenberg's communication derived as much from his resolute, but bipartisan, tone as from the political stance he offered. The Senate had tried since 1943 to establish an international peacekeeping organization, but it wasn't until Vandenberg's speech captured the hearts of the American people that the issue came into focus in the world scene. The stalemate was broken and the Senate approved the United Nations Charter. President Franklin Roosevelt, who now saw Vandenberg as an ally and not an adversary, appointed Vandenberg as a delegate to the first UN conference.

Shared Goals, not Similar Personalities

In 2001, after nearly seven years of work, the "political odd couple," Republican senator John McCain, a war veteran and staunch militarist, and Democratic senator Russ Feingold, grandson of Jewish immigrants and a Rhodes scholar, embraced on the Senate floor. Their bill on campaign finance reform had finally passed. One observer commented that the new law was a "testament to the extraordinary patience and toughness" of

McCain and Feingold. It was also a compliment to a focused and effective communication process that, in order for their work to be successful, required both men to put their attention on their mutual goals rather than on where their ideas diverged.

Talk First, Solve Problems Second

In 2003, San Francisco's district attorney, Kamala Harris, and its police chief, Heather Fong, inherited governmental agencies in which their predecessors had not spoken to each other in years. Awareness of the deep rifts between their departments challenged Fong and Harris to meet regularly (see *Newsweek*, 10/24/05) and to talk through their agencies' difficult conflicts. Working together, they put their communities before their personal and professional agendas. "There are many ways to mediate and defuse situations," said Fong. "Eighty percent of modern policing is about communication, prevention and management." Harris' and Fong's commitment to communicate (and actually talk to each other) has done more than help their agencies move beyond old problems. It also provides a model that all district attorneys and police offers can emulate in working with each other. Good communication at the highest levels resonates throughout government and into the community. It suggests that leaders who can talk to each other can also talk to their constituents.

The Value of SERVE™: An Effective Model for Today's Politicians

Honest communication is the only way that long-lasting, positive social change can occur. When political leaders are able to fully communicate their thoughts, including their highest ideals, they can create a government that supports and provides security for its citizens. Franklin Delano Roosevelt understood this when he spoke out against "fear itself" and established the Works Progress Administration (WPA) and the social security system. McCain and Feingold understood this when they crossed party lines and focused on how to better serve the democratic process rather than on the conflicting beliefs and agendas of their political parties. Harris and Fong understood this when they used respect and achieving mutual goals as foundation for change.

SERVE™ does not ask you to agree with what others say or to take on their beliefs. It enables you to say what you believe in a context that accepts others, their beliefs and actions, and the legislation they propose. At the heart of this model is a basic assumption: If, as political leaders, you can genuinely accept and acknowledge the positive contributions that others make, you can create an environment in which divisive issues can more easily be resolved. This occurs because the focus of your communication can shift from what you *don't* like about others (or what they are doing wrong) to what you *do* like about them (or what they are doing right) and the common ground you share.

Public servants who make use of SERVE™ learn to be less critical of themselves and, therefore, less critical of others. They can focus more on what *is* working and less on what *isn't*, allowing them to build on accomplishments and create momentum for more success. They are also more satisfied with their work and with themselves as leaders.

SERVE™ works because it's based in values, even if you are the only person using it. The values are constant and are yours to rely on repeatedly. For example, if someone insists on focusing on what doesn't work, you can help them move beyond that view by responding with something like, "I have an understanding of what doesn't work. Could you help me understand what does, or would, work?" This simple statement shifts the focus away from the problem and toward the solution.

SERVE™ not only helps you clarify how you want to communicate with others, but it also offers a set of practices that allow you to better serve yourself and others.

10 Ways You Can Serve Yourself and Others

This section will give you an overview of each skill SERVE™ asks you to develop and how your new abilities will benefit your political work. You can develop these abilities at your own pace and/or perfect each skill in more depth with the assistance of a professional coach. The advantage of hiring a coach you trust is that it gives structure to your learning and you gain the benefit of having someone to mirror your accomplishments as you progress.

You don't have to use the model's skills in any particular order. You can use them to prepare yourself for meetings, or you can draw on them while in conversation. After you develop ability with each skill, you will see how they work in relationship with each other. How, little by little, they can become an intrinsic part of your professional and personal communication. Listening deeply and with respect, for example, can remind you that you need to connect with the "heart" of the person you are talking with. It can also remind you to make commitments wisely and take care of yourself.

1. Be Fully Present

Let your mind, body and spirit be wholly focused in the moment to actively participate, acquire new information, or listen differently to information that has come before. Being present shows that you are committed to the communication process and that you care enough about what is being shared to be a genuine part of the process.

2. Maintain Boundaries and Confidentiality

To communicate well in political relationships, you need to know the boundaries of your communication with others—for example, what's confidential and what's not. As you negotiate your boundaries, rely on your core values to remind you of your moral and ethical commitments. Also be aware of your legal responsibilities regarding confidentiality. Opportunities may arise in which you could gain politically by revealing information; but short-term gains can have long-term consequences. Is what you have to share appropriate to reveal to others? Is it confidential? For you to make a positive contribution to others, they have to trust you. Respecting communication boundaries builds that trust.

3. Have a Beginner's Mind

In the beginner's mind, there are many possibilities, but in the expert's mind there are few.
— Jhunryu Suzuki

Having a beginner's mind allows you to approach your communication with a fresh perspective. It can help you learn something new or experience someone in a different way. It can help you implement ideas or solve problems by allowing you to remain open to all information you receive. Being unrestricted allows you to stay flexible and view unorthodox options. A beginner's mind allows you to develop alliances that would otherwise be improbable, and artfully demonstrate that you are committed to being of service to others.

4. Connect at the Heart Level

The Buddhist greeting Namaste is the conscious recognition, acknowledgment, respect and appreciation of the soul or heart of another person. As a leader, when you seek to connect with the heart of a person, you actually deepen your connections with yourself as well as with the other. Allowing people to fully see you, as well as requiring yourself to see them, are an important contribution to the communication process. Namaste offers you the chance to put the "heart" of the person—who they are and what they stand for—before their personality and to bring your own humanness to your communication with them.

5. Listen Deeply and with Honor

When you listen actively, you show other people that you are open to them and that they can trust you. They feel secure and more willing to reveal themselves to you. Psychotherapists learn to listen to content and process—beyond what is being said to how the person is communicating and what they mean.

This is also important in political relationships. When you listen to others, hear the information they have to share, but keep in mind that it's less than 10% of what most people communicate. You must also listen for what they *mean*, what is implied, or what is deliberately not said. Notice what their eyes communicate, how their bodies react, how feelings are shared.

You'll know when someone has really listened to you and you'll feel understood. You'll want to spend more time with that person, no matter what political party they belong to! Remember how you feel when you are listened to and use that feeling to motivate you to listen more carefully to others.

6. Focus on Positive Interactions

Keeping a positive focus means that your attention is on what's working in your communication with another and you are acknowledging it. Marianne Williamson, an internationally acclaimed author, lecturer and founder of The Peace Alliance (a grassroots campaign supporting legislation currently before Congress to establish a US Department of Peace, *www.thepeacealliance.org*, says that what you focus on "expands," meaning that if what you focus on is positive, you'll see more of what's positive around you. This does not signify that you are unaware of all that's going on—just that you're focused on what is going *well*. In the 1990s, marriage and family therapist Dr. John Gottman conducted a study of newlyweds and their behavior. He could predict with 94% accuracy if a marriage would last 10 years. Dr. Gottman discovered that, if a couple averaged five positive interactions to one negative, they would have a strong relationship. What if there were more positive interactions between political leaders who are working together? Can you predict what success they'd have?

7. Take Responsibility

Taking responsibility for yourself is one of the most empowering things you have to rely on when talking with others. Although you may be powerless over specific outcomes, you have complete control over yourself. You can choose what you say and how you say it, what you do, how you receive and respond to information, and how you let things affect you and for how long. You can take things personally and choose to get angry, depressed and frustrated, or you can accept the situation and focus on moving forward. You are responsible for the contribution you make to others.

8. Honor Commitments

The willingness to commit, like the willingness to communicate, evolves from a sense of trust. As a political leader, you want to know that you can follow through and honor your commitments—and you want others to know that too. Ask yourself whether this is a commitment you truly want. What will it require? Can you keep your promise? If necessary, don't respond to requests right away. Make a decision about what you *can* and *want* to do. And commit yourself first. Then you can keep your commitment to others.

9. Give and Receive Constructive Feedback

Providing constructive feedback assures whom you work with that you are genuinely invested and committed to being of service to them. It creates the possibility for "give and take" in the relationship and can help a negotiation, a project or a relationship to move forward. How you provide feedback is also important. Be clear on your intentions, your desire to connect with the whole person, and your positive focus before you deliver what you have to say.

As leaders, you also want to receive constructive feedback from others. When you let people respond to you, or acknowledge you, you encourage them to also reflect on how they communicate. When you let someone recognize you, a mutual connection takes place between you and the other person that fosters trust and fuels the relationship. I also encourage you to acknowledge yourself. Just as we often prefer the gifts we give ourselves, we tend to also like best the credit we give ourselves.

10. Take Care of Yourself

Practice self-care before, during and after communicating with others. When you arrive at a meeting well rested, well fed and in good spirits, you can be more productive. During the meeting, ask for what you need, and do what you need to do to make sure you are able to contribute well. Also, let others take care of themselves. If you notice someone needs something, give them the opportunity to ask for it.

Communication Is the Foundation of Leadership and Service

Jesse Jackson said, "Leadership has a harder job to do than to choose sides. It must bring sides together." To lead successfully in San Francisco, Kamala Harris and Heather Fong knew they could not align with "sides," but had to actually come together and talk to each other. Like Jackson, who has been called "The Great Unifier," they have integrated into their political communication process a commitment to serve others. You must do the same.

SERVE™ makes the "hard job" of political leadership easier by providing a reliable framework you can rely on and return to. It focuses your attention on being of service to others while providing you five essential elements for bringing sides together and moving your political work forward. Communicating effectively in the political process begins with your willingness to reflect on your commitment to service and your desire to speak and act well. By doing so, you can be a leader whom others respond to and trust.

SERVE yourself.
SERVE others.
Just SERVE.

Apply the Insight—SERVE™ in Action	
Be Fully Present	• Set an intention to be fully present. • Show up on time and stay for your section of the meeting. • Avoid unnecessary interruptions. • Consciously focus on the moment. If your mind wanders, gently bring it back to the present. • Avoid alcohol or other mind-altering substances before important conversations or negotiations.
Maintain Boundaries and Confidentiality	• Set an intention to keep boundaries and confidentiality. • Be clear on what is confidential and what you can share with others. • Make a verbal agreement with others to maintain confidentiality. • Refrain from gossip.

Have a Beginner's Mind	• Set an intention to have a beginner's mind. • Don't compare what you are learning to what's come before. • Allow yourself to "try on" the information you receive. You don't have to make decisions or commit to actions. Just "wear" the information in your mind so that you can ultimately make a well-informed decision.
Connect at the Heart Level	• Set an intention to connect with the heart of the person/people you are communicating with. • Hold the person speaking in positive regard, placing principles above personalities. • Let go of the need to evaluate and judge what is being shared.
Listen Deeply and with Honor	• Set an intention to listen deeply and with honor. • Be 100% engaged and focus your attention on the person sharing. • Refrain from side talk, cross talk or interruptions when someone is speaking. Resist making repetitive comments or drawing attention to yourself. • Listen for the essence of what the person is sharing, regardless of the presentation. • Allow the person speaking to indicate that they have finished speaking.
Focus on Positive Interactions	• Set an intention to focus on the interaction itself. • Actively look for what is working and how that can be expanded. • Look for the gifts being shared (the person's vulnerability, authenticity, brilliance).
Take Responsibility	• Set an intention to be responsible in how you speak, act and respond to others. • Speak in "I" statements. Share your experience and claim it. • Look at any choices you are making that might perpetuate an untenable situation. Explore both inner and outer options that could produce more desirable results. • Allow others to be responsible for themselves and resist telling them what they should do, feel or believe. Keep the focus on you.

Honor Commitments	• Set an intention to honor all commitments, including those made to yourself. • Take the time you need before accepting any commitments. Consult your schedule and your heart to see if you are willing and able to follow through. You can always respond with, "Let me get back to you on that" before answering their request. • If you are overcommitted, refrain from self-flogging. Remain in integrity and renegotiate where possible.
Give and Receive Constructive Feedback	• Set an intention to give only constructive feedback and to graciously receive acknowledgments from others. • Maintain eye contact and heart contact with the person you are giving feedback to or who is giving you feedback. • Give advice and suggestions only when asked and only when useful. Notice when you want to give criticism or feedback that really does not serve the person or situation. Then just let it go without utterance. • Be authentic and pose concerns with care. • Keep what you say simple and speak only from personal experience. • Get to the point.
Take Care of Yourself	• Set an intention to practice self-care. • Maintain a safe space for yourself. Take care of your body, mind and spirit. • If you begin to self-judge, simply let the judgment go and choose a new thought and a positive focus. • Empower others by allowing them to take care of themselves.

*Based on the *Standards of Presence in the Inspired Learning Model Handbook*™ published by the Foundation for Inspired Learning, *www.inspiredlearning.org*.

I am grateful to Coach For Life, *www.coachforlife.com,* and the Foundation for Inspired Learning, *www.inspiredlearning.org,* for introducing me to the Standards of Presence and giving me permission to adapt them here for use in the political arena.

The Coaching Journey

Hélène Beauchemin

A coach accompanies you on part of your journey and offers you the opportunity for self-reflection. In addition to challenging your assumptions, a coach will address the ways those assumptions influence your actions and self-image. When leaders are challenged or seduced by power, a coach can reflect back to them the important core values that brought them to public life in the first place.

Political leaders often have a constellation of experts hovering around them: campaign managers, party loyalists, lobbyists, advisors, "policy wonks." This same pattern exists at the uppermost echelons of government, with the added culture of a respect for hierarchy and the ingrained awe reserved for participants in the senior executive boardroom. While these people are usually well-intentioned, their focus—which often has a partisan perspective—is on "protecting their guy" or persuading the political leader to follow their path. Even in the normally apolitical bureaucratic realms, a given program or policy may be defended just as fiercely.

Over time, political leaders can become isolated and begin to believe their own rhetoric. This is where a coach can be invaluable. A coach does not have the same emotional and personal investment in seeing you keep your current position or adhere to past public statements.

We each view the world through the filter of our own experiences and expectations for our future. Power, and proximity to it, can be a powerful drug that begins to distort perspective. History has shown us many people who lost their original path when they were influenced by access to power. In my own career as a political coach, I have seen that political leaders especially can be led astray by those around them; people may confuse their own personal interest with the best interests of the leader. In these realms, loyalty is the top currency. Loyalty, as we were reminded when I was in public service, does not always allow for "speaking truth to power." This is another benefit of working with a professional coach. A top political coach will be totally committed to you and enable you to excel. A coach will have the courage to assist you in facing your dilemmas and keep you from straying from your original core values. As a coach, my focus is on clients achieving results while maintaining their integrity and finding time for their family and personal life.

Other service providers in the leader's entourage bring their own agenda and view of how you should act, talk or dress to retain power that serves them all so well. A coach offers the clarity of distance. We are trained to step back from the immediate issue and remain focused on you. The relationship between client and coach should allow your coach to respectfully voice things that no one else would say. This opens the door to greater integrity for you.

Let me take this opportunity to define what I mean by integrity. In this context, it means staying true to your own values and to what brought you to the world of politics or public service in the first place.

One of the first benefits I bring to my clients is the legitimacy to stop their incredibly busy lives, to step off the treadmill, to take time to think. The exercises and practices I provide can foster discipline in mastering new and more appropriate ways of dealing with life's continuous challenges. A lack of time is one of these challenges.

Another benefit coaching provides you is a safe place to share views, hesitations and concerns. To work in the public service is to live in a demanding and sometimes nasty environment, under continuous public scrutiny. Innuendo and half-truths often evolve into perceived reality. A coach's nonpartisan position provides a confidential place for you to share concerns and develop greater clarity about future actions.

This clarity sometimes includes the realization that the skills and personality traits that served you well in the past are not the ones needed in a new environment. In my role as coach, I assist my clients to observe themselves in action. This allows them to determine which of their skills are no longer useful and how to develop a new set of skills that will ensure their success in their new position of leadership. It enables them to adjust to their new environment.

The coaching relationship presumes a longer commitment than a one-time consultation and, as such, it allows you time to reflect, adapt, create new habits and ways of being, and flex new muscle. Sustained change happens over time, and mastery of new techniques requires a lot of practice. If you were to ask Tiger Woods or Cecilia Bartolli, they would tell you that they excel because they practice and master new strengths and new competencies.

Sometimes taking a break can be somewhat frightening, especially if you are moving full-steam ahead. I know this from personal experience; I've been there. You feel that if you take time out, you will miss something important, or be bypassed and forgotten. You feel that if you manage to get off the treadmill without breaking your neck, you might never get back on again. In this situation, you can lose the ability to distinguish the urgent from the important.

It is essential for clients to set aside time for regular meetings with their coach. But interacting with someone who is talking, walking and (allegedly) thinking at lightning speed is not very productive or credible. My first task with new clients is to get them to stop and breathe. Only then can they realize how to become more effective and be the leaders they need to be.

The fast pace of the world of politics and public policy can make it very tempting. The faster it goes, the more important and essential you feel. But the country doesn't feel joy in knowing that the people making decisions that affect our lives, our health and our world peace are, more often than not, making them "on the fly" while they are multitasking and sleep-deprived.

In the beginning of a coaching relationship with a political leader, I spend most of my time getting them to pause, even if just for a few seconds.

It is only then, when the adrenaline rush has ceased and they have felt the difference, that they can accept that no lasting, well-thought-out policy can come without time for reflection and allowing others to digest the proposals.

When I speak of taking time off, I'm not referring to three weeks in Hawaii, although that would be nice too. I'm referring to something a little more realistic. I have seen a lot of success with a daily practice based on the excellent work of Wendy Palmer (*The Intuitive Body*). I call it the 4-second 4-step. I recommend you do it at least 20 times a day. In total, it takes less than 90 seconds, but it provides 20 opportunities each day to take a deep breath, become conscious of things, and realize who and where you are. In those 90 seconds, you can determine what is really important and make conscious choices about your actions. Recently someone said to me, "I realize now that I want to make the distinction between dealing with anxieties and dealing with important matters." Good reflection.

The coach creates a safe space for you to relax, rejuvenate and recharge before moving out into the world again, ready to give it your best. A good coach also ensures that you don't become dependent on the coaching relationship. Your coach will provide the tools and skills to allow you to observe, correct and regenerate yourself in the future. I can't count the number of leaders who have told me that one of the most valuable things they gained from coaching was the necessity to block off an hour. It enabled them to tell everyone to go away, to have a safe space to be heard, to reflect and even admit some fears that they could then work out for themselves before going back into the fray.

Being centered is crucial. Imagine being pulled in all directions (or maybe you don't have to imagine it—maybe you're living it), and being briefed on important issues while you're in an elevator or a car bringing you to the House just before a vote. A coach offers you ways to master these situations, to become centered in the moment without letting other things interfere. This brings clarity as well as serenity and allows for more deliberate and thoughtful decision making.

Of course, everyone has a personal rhythm of change, so your coach won't impose a pace on you. Coaches don't expect anyone else to function at their rhythm but, at the same time, they recognize that people are protesting change because they don't want to move out of their comfort zone. If you are resisting change, your coach should nudge you into the unknown, where growth will occur. Usually, the longer someone has been doing something a certain way, the longer it takes them to change and create new habits. I often recall the words of James Flaherty, founder of New Ventures West school of coaching: "Change occurs in biological time."

The path to success is often clear only in hindsight—after you have achieved your goals. While you may wonder why you didn't catch things earlier, they weren't evident to you then—there was no catching to be done. Coaching is an iterative process. So is life, if you think about it. I could spend time looking back and wishing I had used my current knowledge with a past client. But that is silly because they are different times.

Of course, there will be times when your coach is affected by your public policies. As such, a professional coach has the integrity and self-knowledge to be aware when there is a risk of crossing the line into projecting a personal agenda. If the apparent conflict of interest could be too great, a good coach will advise you to hire someone else.

Being the Ideal Client

Who are the ideal political clients for coaching? People who accept that they are on a learning journey. People with the desire to build on who they have been and what they have accomplished, who want to learn to create the improvements they need to achieve their personal vision for their countrymen.

In this book, we use "political leader" to identify someone who intends to impact public policy. They may be elected officials, community activists, lobbyists, appointees or public servants. The leaders most appropriate for coaching have not yet built so thick a shell around themselves that they can't be reached or touched. There must at least be a crack in the armour to allow entry for the coach.

To be a good coaching client, you must be ready to learn more about yourself and have a desire for growth and excellence. You must want to move toward growth and away from failure or breakdowns. You must be willing to move out of the status quo. You must have the courage to allow your vulnerability to show.

There are always breakdown moments—times of great disappointment, defeat or crisis, like losing an election or not getting legislation passed—that can create opportunities conducive to coaching. A coach can assist with the healing process and support you as you grow from it, IF you are willing to let yourself be true.

Conversely, coaching opportunities can come in moments of euphoria: when you attain that new job or post, when you feel on top of the world and have the lucidity to ask yourself, "Now that I'm here, how will I succeed and still remain true to my core values?"

Even without such a watershed moment, coaching opportunities can arise from just feeling stuck or feeling that the passion is missing from your work. There is no one rule that defines the ideal coaching client. The only rule that matters is this: You must have a willingness to look at yourself, you must be willing to learn, and you must put these lessons into practice in order to increase in excellence.

Let me be perfectly clear about this: There does not need to be a crisis for coaching to be useful. Some clients use coaching to make sure they stay at the top of their game and even take it up a notch. I mention crisis situations because, in those moments, the stage is set for looking at new ways of achieving success, since the old ways evidently did not work.

Coaching is *not* about fixing. Humans don't need to be fixed. Situations, maybe, but not people. Another important distinction is that coaches are not therapists or trainers. Coaching is about building the skills necessary to move forward and gain excellence professionally. The perception of coaching has changed in many circles: many political leaders now see coaching as one of the perks of the job. Most top leaders, by the time they reach that position, have had numerous courses in leadership, management theories, change management and such. They do not need more classes.

Coaching Democracy:
Lessons from the Longhouse

Dennis S. Brogan

Here's an interesting point about democracy: Europeans did not bring it to America. We may have adapted it, but democracy has been in the Americas for many centuries. When they searched for a path toward the formation of our nation and government, our founders sought out coaches from a people with 600 years of democratic experience, making coaching a crucial element in the foundation of our modern democracy.

I believe the Iroquois were the first executive coaches in America. According to a *National Geographic* article, and confirmed by Chief Oren Lyons, the Native Americans' representative to the United Nations, many Iroquois chiefs were brought to Lancaster and Philadelphia, Pennsylvania; Albany and New York City, New York, as respected leaders. As early as 1744, the Iroquois were called on by our forefathers to explain their government, a role we would now characterize as coaches or consultants. The Articles of Confederation, agreed to by Congress on November 15, 1777, and ratified on March 1, 1781, was modeled after the Iroquois Confederacy—autonomous states joined in the common thread of democracy.

Thomas Jefferson wrote, in *Defense of the Constitution of the United States,* that we should use the Iroquois' fifty families as a model for Americans to follow. In a speech to Colonial governors in Lancaster,

Canasetoga, the Iroquois Tadadaho, encouraged our union to be confederacy of states. The following quote was recorded by a future framer of our nation and laws, Benjamin Franklin:

> Our wise forefathers established union and amity between the Five Nations. This has made us formidable; this has given us great weight and authority with our neighboring nations. We are a powerful confederacy, and by your observing the same methods our wise forefathers have taken, you will acquire such strength and power. Therefore, whatever befalls you, never fall out with one another.

Other stories tell of several great Iroquois chiefs coming to New York City and attending Congress. They explained to the leaders, who were trying to maintain physical order, that you can't scream down your opponent in the longhouse (meeting hall), that everyone has a voice to be heard, and that there must be no physical attacks. Today, the hate and distance between opposing sides on issues in Washington and our hometowns truly divides our nation and people. We need to remember Canasetoga's statement, "Whatever befalls you, never fall out with one another."

The Iroquois not only provided a model and human rights laws that seemed to have influenced Jefferson, Adams and Franklin, but a nation as well and, in doing so, the world. Years later, the Clan Mothers of the Iroquois worked closely with Susan B. Anthony, Matilda Joslyn Gage, Elizabeth Cady Stanton and other advocates to further women's rights. On September 16, 1987, the 100th Congress acknowledged the Iroquois' influence on our development into a government by and of the people.

Today, the Iroquois Confederacy still meets in their longhouse, located just two miles, as the crow flies, from where I sit. Not long ago, this native land was the only one recognized as sovereign by our government. To this day, American officials must ask permission to enter the Onondaga Nation, where they still meet as a confederacy of confederacies, honoring their ancestral traditions. Theirs was the first form of democracy in the Western Hemisphere.

The Iroquois' story is a rich history of the beginnings of executive coaches. The Iroquois contributed to the context, or foundation, of our democracy by sharing the principles of the Iroquois Confederacy. The Iroquois coached our founders to explore and create our own government. They helped our founders further this democratic journey; this is where executive coaching started in America.

To understand the Iroquois' motivation in assisting our fledgling nation, we return to 1142 AD on the shores of Onondaga Lake in Syracuse, New York, when the Peacemaker, Dekanawidah, first made known the concept that every decision should be made looking forward seven generations. The Iroquois represent one essence of integrity, and their thought of looking forward seven generations should echo through the halls of Washington and your town. At the 2005 International Coach Federation's annual conference, the ICF President, Steve Mitten, spoke of this key Native American belief. He called for coaching, as a profession and as individual coaches, to act as stewards of next-seven-generation thinking, just as the Clan Mothers of the Iroquois have for scores of generations, and through them, for the founders of the United States.

The power of the Iroquois did not lie in force, but rather in choice. They did not force our founders to follow their model; instead they offered it and encouraged our founders to make their own choices, in the same manner as a coach works with a client.

As a result of these choices, there are subtle, yet monumental, differences in our two democratic governments. One example is when the Clan Mothers are looking for a new chief, they don't have to look far, for they have raised the new leader, as they raise all their chiefs, and in doing so have coached them to find their greatness. The Clan Mothers don't necessarily choose the male who *wants* to be chief; they choose someone who will pass the consensus of the clan. They look for the male who does not *need* to lead, but has the wisdom of many generations before him. They operate from a view of seven generations forward and, from what we can tell, at least seven generations past as well. Their leadership development is not haphazard; they grow their leaders.

Currently in the United States, the leaders we grow on a national level are often disconnected from the core of American voters. Not much is driven by consensus anymore. Most decisions are driven by the next election cycle. To serve our core citizenry, as well as the fringe of the nation, leaders must work more in the consensus model.

The most important outcome of the 2006 general election was that voters made a clear statement to local, state and federal officials. No longer would we accept partisan and muckraking politics. The voters forced the change and direction of the political culture to serve the middle of America, thereby putting the American people before any political party.

How does this event relate to the moment and the next seven generations? It is all about leadership!

Leadership is the courage to admit mistakes, the vision to welcome change, the enthusiasm to motivate others, and the confidence to stay out of step when everyone else is marching out of tune.
— Former Telecom CEO

This is the most brilliant quote I have ever come across describing the essence of leadership. The confidence to admit mistakes, a wide view to welcome and support change, and the energy and enthusiasm to motivate not only yourself but those whose paths you cross. This is the work of present-day executive coaches.

Every politician who hires a political consultant when running for office should hire a coach the day prior. If you are a senior staff person or an elected official, being centered in your integrity and the values that called you to political office need to ring true. The consultant will tell you how to beat the other candidate through polling and strategy; the coach will help you maintain the person you need to be to attract voters to your message and passion for serving.

It is also important to become an excellent manager of the people surrounding you, from the consultant to the grassroots political volunteer who knocks on doors to assist you in getting the vote out. Plenty of consultants will tell you how you should put together your staff; coaches support you in taking a consultant's template and make it your own.

Companies like Boeing, MCI, IBM, Bristol-Myers Squibb, the United States government agencies, and others are using internal and external coaching supports to improve performance and results. Many state, local and federal employees are also receiving coaching services in some form. Politicians should follow suit. A coaching program for political leaders can help politicians and senior staff gain confidence in their political leadership skills, build the courage to make mistakes, be able to share your vision for all to hear, and help citizens be empowered by your goals. In addition, political leadership is quickly evolving and changing. Politicians must learn to be coaches themselves—mentoring their constituents and others, leading their staffs, and returning to the primary core values that we all share. It's common sense for the common good.

The funny thing about common sense is it ain't all that common.
—Mark Twain

At a recent event recognizing the Iroquois contributions to our founding and nation, I had the privilege and opportunity to speak with the current Tadadaho of the Iroquois, Chief Sid Hill. As we spoke and listened to Clan Mother Estelle Gibson, the message I gained was one of returning the United States to our democratic roots and to our varied foundations of democracy to create the possibilities for the generation living here today and for seven generations more...and beyond.

Sourcing:
The essay entitled "Coaching for Democracy" consists of observations and discussions with Chief Sid Hill and Chief Oren Lyons, the Native Americans' representative to the United Nations and their ambassador to the world. A professor at the University of Buffalo, Chief Lyons has taught American history and ecology during his 36-year tenure. A former All-American lacrosse player, artist and environmental activist and leader, Chief Lyons is a man of knowledge and faith. We have had many conversations about the Iroquois, the earth and democracy. In the Iroquois culture, history is passed on verbally through stories, and very little is written down. Chief Lyons dreams of creating the Center for Western Democracy on the shores of Onondaga Lake where world leaders would journey to further democracy and human rights.

INDEX

Author Biographies

Hélène Beauchemin, PCC
HKBP, Inc.
Ottawa, Canada
613.236.4847
helene@hkbp.ca

Hélène Beauchemin is president of HKBP, Inc., a management consulting firm for senior leaders seeking executive coaching and professional and personal development. She is a professionally certified integral coach trained at New Ventures West in San Francisco.

Because she has worked at senior levels in government, Hélène has the gift of demystifying leadership. Having spent many years working with provincial and federal governments in positions including assistant deputy minister, she is able to offer her clients coaching from her wealth of experience. She shows parliamentarians, seasoned executives, board members and association executives the best practices for being a leader people will want to follow and work for.

Executives at all levels need to enhance their skills and learn to read and understand a new environment. They turn to Hélène for help in honing these skills because they know she's lived it. "I've moved 36 times in my life; I've learned to quickly read an environment and culture."

She now resides in Ottawa, Ontario, Canada. She and husband Peter have a reconstituted family of two sons, three daughters and a dozen grandchildren, as well as a classic wooden motor cruiser that is their cottage on the water.

Dennis S. Brogan
WINS Coaching Services
Syracuse, New York
315.382.4437
dennisb.newtonproducts@gmail.com

Dennis Brogan is a journeyman in business and service. He worked in broadcast radio as a morning radio cohost, sales executive and senior manager for nearly 20 years. His varied leadership roles include director of sales and development for Ryan Communications, a role where he oversaw an annual marketing and advertising budget of over $8 million dollars for Carrier Corporation's Enterprise Division. Dennis currently works at the executive level of local government as a senior staff member to Matthew J. Driscoll, mayor of the City of Syracuse.

A successful entrepreneur, Dennis also operates WINS Coaching Services, a business management, leadership and coaching service. His work includes coaching political and governmental leaders. Dennis is a member of the International Coach Federation.

In 2005, he started Newton Business Programs with Edward Rogoff, PhD. Newton Business Programs designs and delivers training and inspirational and communications programs for a variety of clients to support their growth and development. Dennis is also a commissioner of human rights in Syracuse, New York; a founding board member of the Syracuse International Film and Video Festival, the founding president of Rebuilding Together with Christmas in April in Syracuse and Binghamton, New York; a trustee of the Landmark Theater, and president and CEO of Good Karma Koffee Company and Importing.

Dennis has two beautiful daughters, Colleen and Meghan, to whom his contribution to this book is dedicated. Dennis is an avid outdoorsman, sailor and woodworker.

Anne Long Fifield, CPCC
New York, New York
718.722.7571
anne@annefifield.com

Anne Fifield is a Co-active Professional Certified Coach and an independent communications strategist. For more than 15 years, she has worked with leaders and entrepreneurs in media, advertising, finance, and technology. Anne is known for her creativity, her passionate commitment to clarity, and her ability to handle complicated situations and information in ways that promote rapport. She has been selected to work on complex and sensitive assignments with cultural and non-profit institutions such as The Pope John Paul II Cultural Center, the National Museum for Civil Rights, The Pioneer Institute, and the Military Academy at West Point.

A graduate of Princeton University, Anne has taught strategic communications at The City University of New York (CUNY). Her private coaching clients include accomplished solo artists, entrepreneurs, and competitive athletes.

Erika Gabaldon, MA, ACC
Glass Houses Coaching & Consulting, Inc.
Los Angeles, California
866.517.7291
erika@glasshousescoaching.com

Erika Gabaldon, president of Glass Houses Coaching & Consulting, Inc., serves people in the public eye, including political leaders, celebrities, sports figures, business executives, and clients' families and staffs. Credentialed through the International Coach Federation (ICF) and certified through Coach For Life, Erika offers life coaching and management consulting to help those who reside in the "glass houses" of public life to prepare, develop and thrive.

Erika is also trained as an Inspired Learning Facilitator through the Foundation for Inspired Learning (San Diego, CA) and holds a master's degree in Spiritual Psychology from the University of Santa Monica (Santa Monica, CA). She is a member of ICF (national and Los Angeles) and the Screen Actors Guild. She also serves on the advisory board of Young Progressive Majority (YPM), a social network of 20-30 year olds committed to increasing the vote for local progressive candidates and issues.

Erika is a true "democracy geek"; when she is not working, you'll find her reading books or articles on American politics, attending leadership conferences, or participating in political gatherings, activities and events. Erika lives in Los Angeles with her husband, Spike Feresten.

Samuel P.B. House, MCC
Soulutions Leadership and Consulting
Delmar, New York
518.475.7813
sam@soulutionsleadership.com

Sam House, president of Soulutions Leadership and Consulting, is a Master Certified Coach and a leadership consultant. For over 20 years, he has engaged in bringing out the best in others in his roles as a coach, a leader/facilitator, and as a therapist. As a senior faculty member for the Coaches Training Institute—the largest coaching training organization in the world—Sam has worked with emerging leaders in the top Fortune 100 companies. He designs and delivers programs that result in high team effectiveness and full-permission leadership at all levels of an organization. In addition, he provides intensive and experientially based leadership training in northern California, Europe, and Asia for leaders across the globe.

Heather Cummings Jensen, CPCC
Conscious Politics
Athens, Georgia
706.534.5023
heather@heathercummings.com

Heather Cummings' work as an executive coach is an outgrowth of her deeply held values and her caring for the world.

In 1993, she attended the World Conference on Human Rights and, as a delegate of Rights of Women, London, she contributed to the final NGO Declaration. Fascinated by international politics, Heather traveled on a train chartered by the Women's International League for Peace and Freedom that stopped in St. Petersburg, Kiev, Bucharest, Sofia, Istanbul, Odessa, Almaty and Beijing. At each stop, she met with local women leaders in business and politics. At this time—1995—it became clear to her that the world is connected and that the policies of the West have impact around the world and vice versa.

While she had profound interest and caring about international politics, she recognized that the best way she could serve was to help her country "take care of its own backyard." Still, she wasn't clear about how she would do that until she became a professional coach after a successful career in the corporate world.

Heather recognized that there is an emerging need in the American political system for a structure that supports leaders in reflecting on the issues at hand, assessing them in light of their values, and consciously deciding on the next steps for their political leadership. To provide this structure for those in public service, Heather shifted the focus of her coaching practice to working with political leaders. For this reason Heather co-founded Southern Truth and Reconciliation.

Heather graduated cum laude from Occidental College, Los Angeles, with a degree in women's studies and an emphasis in politics. Heather is accredited through the International Coach Federation and is certified by the Coaches Training Institute.

Betsy Corley Pickren, M.Ed., PCC, CPCC
Facilitated Learning, Inc.
Duluth, Georgia
770.263.7736
betsy@facilitatedlearninginc.com

Betsy Corley Pickren is president of Facilitated Learning, Inc., which focuses on promoting healthy, vibrant leaders and teams in organizations. Clients include: Turner Broadcasting, Cox Communications, the State Merit System of Georgia, the US Department of Agriculture, Emory University Libraries and CompuCredit. Betsy has a special interest in supporting people in elected public office to lead with authenticity, integrity and courage.

From 1982 to 1995, Betsy was an associate with Zenger-Miller, one of the nation's largest leadership development firms, where she trained facilitators in Fortune 100 companies, government agencies and international organizations. As vice president for Client Services, Betsy's segment of the company served the needs of more than 3,000 clients. Betsy also has firsthand experience on the "client side" through in-house management positions in banking and government. She was a member of the Carter-Mondale Transition Team and later was supervisor of Presidential personnel for The White House.

Betsy began her career as a high school teacher in Gwinnett County, Georgia, where she was named "Star Teacher." Her interest in the continued vitality of political leadership can be attributed to the fact that both her father and grandfather served as county commissioners.

She has been active in a variety of community and professional organizations. A mentor for PathBuilders (a mentoring program for women leaders in business), she has also served as past president of the Georgia Coach Association and co-chair for the first annual Atlanta PRISM Awards, which celebrate excellence in coaching in organizations.

Betsy earned a master's degree in Adult Education Program Management from Georgia State University. She is certified by the Coaches Training Institute, and credentialed as a Professional Certified Coach through the International Coach Federation.

Michelle Randall, MBA, PCC, CPCC
Glass Houses Coaching & Consulting, Inc.
Morgan Hill, California
866.517.7291
michelle@glasshousescoaching.com

Michelle Randall is CEO of Glass Houses Coaching & Consulting, Inc., which serves people in the public eye. Their clientele includes political leaders, celebrities, sports figures, business executives, and their families and staff. Services include executive coaching and management consulting to help prominent people to identify and express their legendary leadership.

Prior to cofounding the company, Michelle was the principal and lead executive coach for The Juncture Company, which specialized in leadership development and corporate training. Michelle has worked as an executive in both the high-tech and construction industries, where her specialty was new market development. In high-tech, she ran the marketing function and launched both a company and its innovative product. Michelle was a pioneer in sustainable business, introducing the first green-building product line at a mainstream supplier. She went on to serve in the novel position of director of sustainability, encompassing values-based leadership of marketing, finance and operational activities.

Michelle's experience spans the globe, from working with CEOs from Asia, Africa, Europe and the US, to sharing black-market vodka with young leaders of change in the Soviet Union. She lived in Germany for years, and for part of that time managed international business contacts for the CEO and vice president international at Deutsche Telecom, the world's third largest telecommunications company. Michelle earned a Master of Business Administration at the Monterey Institute of International Studies, and a Bachelor of Arts from Eleanor Roosevelt College at the University of California, San Diego. She is a graduate of the Coaches Training Institute, a Professional Certified Coach, and a member of the International Coach Federation.

Chad White, MBA
The Gumption Partners
Athens, Georgia
408.782.1703
chad@brauercapital.com

The Gumption Partners is a collaboration between Chad White and Michelle Randall that specializes in interventions repairing communication among city council members through an emphasis on personal leadership.

This partnership exhibits true bipartisanship between a dyed-in-the-wool Democrat and a committed Republican who regularly engage in passionate policy discussions. The gloves are off, but there is always an underlying mutual respect and commitment to solving issues that make a difference to their families, businesses, community and world.

Chad White is a consultant in turnaround management. He is the managing partner of a private equity firm that invests in underperforming companies. Chad holds a BSE in biomedical engineering from Duke University and a Masters of Business Administration from Vanderbilt University, and he has completed the requirements for a Masters of Science in Taxation at Georgia State University. In addition, he is a member of the MLF Client Office, which consults and assists wealthy families with the challenges and opportunities of wealth transfer between generations through leadership and stewardship.